JACOB'S DAUGHTER

Book 1

WRITTEN BY
Samantha Jillian Bayarr

Samantha Jillian Bayarr
    Jacob's Daughter **27 Chapters**
PLUS two bonus chapters at the end of this book of
Amish Winter Wonderland: Book Two

Also by Samantha Jillian Bayarr

LWF Amish Series
Little Wild Flower Book I
Little Wild Flower Book II
The Taming of a Wild Flower
Little Wild Flower in Bloom
Little Wild Flower's Journey

Christian Romance
Milk Maid in Heaven
The Anniversary

Christian Historical Romance
A Sheriff's Legacy: Book One
Preacher Outlaw: Book Two
Cattle Rustler in Petticoats: Book Three

Jacob's Daughter Amish Collection
Jacob's Daughter
Amish Winter Wonderland
Under the Mulberry Tree
Amish Winter of Promises
Amish Summer of Courage
An Amish Harvest
An Amish Christmas Wish

Companion Series
An Amish Courtship
The Quilter's Son
An Amish Widower
Amish Sisters

**Please note: All editions may not be available yet.
Please check online for availability.**

CHAPTER 1

"I'm what?"

"You heard me, Abby. Now hurry up and put this dress over your head before we miss our bus."

Lizzie Barlow stood her ground. She could feel no sympathy for her daughter at the moment. They had to get on that bus to Indiana, and there was no time for the temper-tantrums of a ten-year-old to complicate their already life-threatening situation.

"I'm not Amish! You take that back!"

Lizzie pursed her lips. "Actually, Abby, you *are* Amish because *I'm* Amish."

Abby placed her hands on her hips in defiance.

"I'm not Amish! Why do I have to dress like them?"

Lizzie shushed her daughter, who was practically screaming.

She stamped her feet. "I want to go home right now!"

Lizzie firmly grasped her daughter by her arms and forced her to look at her. "We don't live there anymore. We have to go to Indiana. We'll make a new life there, and you'll love it so much you'll never want to leave."

Tears pooled in Abby's eyes. "If it's so great in Indiana, then why did you leave?"

The question pricked Lizzie's heart, and she was growing impatient with her daughter.

"It's complicated, Abby."

"Is it because of my father?"

Tears streamed down her cheeks, and Lizzie bit her lower lip to keep from giving in to her child's whims.

"We are *not* having this conversation right now. We're running out of time. Get dressed and we can talk once we arrive safely in Indiana."

"Why do we have to wear these awful clothes, Mom?"

Lizzie looked in the faded mirror in the bathroom of the bus depot, trying to wipe the remaining makeup from her face. "They aren't awful. And we're wearing them so Eddie's friends won't notice us if they should come looking."

"But I wanna wear my Hello Kitty shirt!"

Lizzie sighed. "Please don't make this harder than it already is, Abby. Slip this dress over your head, and hurry before we miss the bus."

She'd begun making the Amish dresses secretly, being careful to hide them from Eddie, Abby's drug-addicted father, so they would have them for their escape. Finding out he was Abby's father only three months ago, he'd threatened Lizzie that he'd kill her and take Abby if she wouldn't give him large sums of money to pay off his debt and support his drug habit. Lizzie didn't intend to stick around long enough to find out how much worse the situation with him would get. For weeks, she'd planned her escape from Eddie's threats, until the day he was found dead from a drug-induced, car accident that totaled Lizzie's car.

Dating him only two short weeks when she was still only seventeen, Lizzie tried to convince herself he was "the one" when they'd met, but she knew deep down she needed to end it with him so they could keep the passion between them respectable because he was a pushy *Englischer*. Sadly, she knew she could never really love him as much as a person ought to in order to take their relationship to the next level. She'd given her heart to only one man in her life, and she knew she could never feel that way for another. But when Eddie took advantage of her, she was left pregnant and ran from him.

Despite changing her name, Eddie still managed to locate her. And that's when the threats began. He demanded money from her to keep quiet about being Abby's father, and started threatening her when she wouldn't give him any more. Trying to spare her daughter from knowing the ugly truth of how she came into the world, she gave in to Eddie's threats until she just couldn't take it anymore.

Lizzie didn't make much money as a pharmacy technician, and when Eddie learned of her employment after coming into the pharmacy to try to redeem an illegal prescription for pain meds, he tried to force her to steal prescription medications for him. Out of fear of what he might do, she'd promised him she would do it, even though she had never stolen anything in her life, and she wasn't about to start. She'd managed to keep him at bay for a couple of days by telling him she hadn't found a way around the cameras in the pharmacy, but when he began showing up at her job, threatening her and her fellow employees, Lizzie was fired. It was too late for her to wish she'd moved farther away from him than the next small town over.

That same day, Eddie stormed out of the pharmacy in a rage of anger, and then totaled her car that he'd been *borrowing* by running it into the side of a tree, ending his battle with drugs—and his life.

Lizzie hadn't even cried. It wasn't that she was heartless, or didn't care that he'd died—she'd done her crying ten years earlier when she decided to leave him after he violated her. In truth, it was over between them the day that he drugged her and stole her innocence.

Still, she could feel little more than relief that her nightmare with him would be put to rest along with his remains. Though Eddie's pain and suffering was ended, her anger over the mountain of debt she was left with due to his reckless behavior had all but destroyed her. Not to mention the threats from the men who wanted her only child in exchange for a debt she didn't owe.

Because she'd let her car insurance policy lapse to give money to Eddie, she was stuck with a car that was no longer drivable, but was still responsible for the payment. And when those thugs started threatening her over the money that Eddie had borrowed from them and for drugs he had never paid for, Lizzie knew it was time to leave this life of debt and pain behind—for Abby's sake—and for her own peace of mind. Her mistakes in judgment had caused her ten-year-old daughter more harm than she was capable of understanding at her young age, and Lizzie knew what she had to do; it was time for her to face the sins of her past, and suffer the consequences to spare Abby from being caught in the middle of her poor choices any longer.

Losing her job, her car, and the threats from the drug-dealers all in a week's time was too much for Lizzie to handle. She'd seen the men before, and even witnessed them roughing Eddie up one night outside of her small, rented house. That's when she heard him promise them Lizzie could get them drugs. And that's when she decided the only way to get away from the thugs that were threatening her was to continue her original plan and find a place to hide from Eddie's mistakes; a place no one would ever think to look for her.

The Amish community.

No one knew of Lizzie's past—not even her own daughter. Given the nature of the events that prompted her to flee from the only way of life she'd ever known, she determined over the years to keep her past hidden, and had even practiced continuously to lose her German accent, and pattern her life after the *Englisch*. She determined, however, to maintain the teachings of her upbringing–even if only in secret. So far, she'd managed to keep her past hidden all these years, and now she was about to walk right back into it with Abby in tow.

Lizzie pulled the plain shoes and stockings from the backpack where she'd kept them hidden for weeks, and handed a pair to her daughter. "Put these on. We have to hurry and pin your hair up in the back."

Abby was busy texting her friends, probably telling them how unfair her only parent was being at the moment, and Lizzie knew it was going to be an even bigger argument when she broke the news to her daughter that the phone would soon be turned off due to non-payment. She reminded herself that it was for the best, since she wouldn't take any chances that Eddie's drug-dealing friends could use the device to track them down. She would have to wait for a while to get a new phone; necessities were the only thing they had money for until Lizzie could find a new job.

She would also worry about getting a cheap car once they got to Indiana; she would use a portion of the money she'd gotten from selling all of their things on Craig's List. She would need a car to look for work so she could find a small house to rent for her and Abby to start over.

Lizzie pulled her hair up and twisted it at the base of her neck, pinning it in place. She placed a prayer *kapp* over her head and handed the other one to Abby.

"Where did you get these weird hats?"

"They're called *prayer kapps*, and I made them."

"How do you know how to make this stuff?"

"YouTube has a video for everything; you know that." She wasn't exactly lying. YouTube did have a how-to video for practically everything, but Lizzie already knew how to make the *prayer kapps*, but she wasn't ready to tell Abby the entire story of her past just yet. She would save it for when they were far enough away from Ohio that she could relax enough to tell her everything.

When they were completely dressed in their disguises, Lizzie took one last look in the mirror. She never intended to wear Plain clothing again—let alone to walk back into Amish territory, but it was out of necessity that she would brave this move.

Without makeup, Lizzie thought she looked well beyond the twenty-eight years that she was, and getting pregnant at seventeen had not helped matters. It was more likely that all the hardship of the past years had aged her. Deep down, she knew some fresh air and a good dose of home-cooking was all it would take, and she'd be good as new.

As they exited the bus depot restroom, Lizzie looked over her shoulder to make sure no one had followed her and Abby. Just a few more minutes and they would be on the bus and on their way to Indiana where Eddie's *friends* would never suspect to look for them.

She *had* to go back home.

It was her only chance of escaping from her life with Eddie for good. Lizzie's own mother had died when she was Abby's age, and if her father had known about Abby, he would have shunned her. It was probably the best thing for her at the time to assume she'd been shunned, since it forced her to grow up and go to college. But even her education couldn't save her now from the damage Eddie had done.

They boarded the bus, but only when it pulled away from the depot, did Lizzie begin to relax a little. Their immediate future was unsure, but her destination for now, was the Miller Bed and Breakfast just off County Road 27, near the home where she grew up.

CHAPTER 2

Jacob Yoder tossed the basin full of water out the barn door, and put a hand to his freshly shaved chin. His skin felt funny after having worn the beard for the past ten years, but it was time to end his mourning period for Nellie. They'd been married only ten months before she died, and Jacob had suffered more with the guilt that he'd married her on the rebound, than with the pain of losing a wife that was dear to him. His guilt only magnified when she died giving birth to his son, Caleb. She was a good woman and did not deserve the fate she'd been dealt when she married him. The only good thing to come from their marriage was Caleb, and it was time for Jacob to try to put the sins of his past behind him—for Caleb's sake. He would no longer hold onto the past or wish for what could have been; he would honor his *fraa's* memory and do right by their son.

He married Nellie when he was just eighteen years old, even though he was still in love with Lizzie. He and Lizzie had been best friends since they were ten years old. Her father had refused to allow her to court like other girls her age. So they did what most of the Amish teenagers did at the time, and saw each other secretly. Being the only daughter of Hiram Miller, Lizzie's activities were constantly monitored by her two older brothers, especially after her *mamm* had died from complications after miscarrying a child that came along unexpectedly when Lizzie was only ten years old.

Despite the strict ties on Lizzie, she and Jacob still managed to sneak in some time together, until her *bruder*, David, caught them and reported back to her father. From that day on, they were forbidden to see each other again. Because of the risk of seeing each other and getting caught, Jacob longed for the day she would turn eighteen and marry him. But when her *bruder,* David came to him with the news that she no longer wanted to see him, he was devastated.

One month later, Jacob began to court Nellie, and Lizzie ran off with some *Englisch* friends. It had broken his heart to learn that she'd left Indiana after sending word with her *bruder,* David that she no longer wanted to see him just a few short weeks before, but his future with Nellie was already set in motion. If only she'd had the guts to say it to his face, he might have had the chance to talk her out of her decision.

Jacob pushed the memories away, putting them back where he'd kept them for the past ten years—locked away in his numb heart, where he refused to let himself feel them. Lizzie was his past, and he needed to stop thinking about her. He had several acres of corn that needed to be harvested, and a young son that was itching to learn to be just like his *daed*. Jacob had spent too many years thinking that the sins of his past were responsible for his *fraa's* death. But now, he was determined to put all of it behind him and be the best father the boy could have.

Caleb wandered sleepily into the barn, the sun barely up. He took a step back at the sight of Jacob standing before him—beardless. "*Daed*, is that you?"

"*Jah*, I shaved my *baard*."

It was an outward sign to end his mourning period, but it wouldn't quiet the guilt that had eaten away at him for so many years. That was something he would have to work on to get rid of—for Caleb's sake.

Caleb thought about it for a minute and then looked to the ground. "Does this mean you will be getting married again? When Jonah Beiler's *daed* shaved his *baard*, he got married, and now Jonah has a new *mamm*."

Jacob put a hand on top of his son's head and gave his thick, blonde hair a shake. "You're not getting a new *mamm*, and I'm not getting married."

Caleb smiled up at Jacob. "It wouldn't be so bad having a *mamm*."

Jacob sighed. He didn't intend to get married again, despite the fact that there were presently two women his age in the community who never married. He'd gone to school with both of them as a young boy, but had never had any other contact with them since. They'd attended church services and community outings, but Jacob never paid them any mind because he had no reason to consider them for anything other than part of a working community—no matter how much prompting he'd had from friends and family to take a second look at them.

Jacob's only focus now would be his son and his farm. If the sudden change in weather would be any indication of the winter ahead of them, he would need to bring in his crop in record time. He knew the task would easily be accomplished with the help of his family and neighbors. He was happy that Caleb was taking an active interest in the harvest, and Jacob was determined to teach him to be a good farmer. Though he didn't want to add to the chores the boy already did, he knew that he needed the experience if he was to take over his father's land one day.

Knowing the single women of the community would attend the harvest, Jacob was suddenly wary of his decision to shave off his beard so soon. It had been a shield for Jacob for the past ten years, and now the entire community would think he was in the market for a *fraa*—especially with wedding season upon them. Panic filled him, and he whispered a short prayer while Caleb ran off to feed the chickens.

Just as he ended his prayer, Jacob could hear the clip-clop of the horses pulling buggies full of the *menner* who were traveling up the lane to begin the harvest. Soon, the day would be underway, and the men would bring in the crops while the women prepared food and visited.

Jacob put a hand to his chin and rubbed at the bare skin. It was too late to rethink his decision, but it wasn't too late to guard his heart against any of the women who would show an interest in him. He would have to keep his eyes toward the ground when the food was served, and he would keep his company contained to that of the men in the community. Even though he'd been a widower for ten years, there had been room in his heart for only one woman, and he had never found room for any other—not even for his own *fraa*.

CHAPTER 3

Lizzie stepped off the bus in Elkhart, Indiana, feeling full of hope for the first time in months. Though she knew it would be a challenge to be in her old stomping ground after so many years, she was excited to see her Aunt Bess again. It wouldn't be the same as seeing her *daed* or her *brieder*, but with her aunt running the B&B, it would be easier to blend in since she catered to the *Englisch*. She wondered if her aunt would accept her as an *Englischer* after all these years, but the phone conversations they'd had recently gave Lizzie hope that she would be able to make the transition easier for Abby. Not only would it be easier for her to have help from a family member, but she looked forward to introducing her daughter to her aunt, and finally telling Abby of her family history.

The only thing that made her nervous about her decision to go back home, was the possibility of running into Jacob Yoder. Surely he was married by now with several *kinner,* and she wasn't certain how that would make her feel. Probably jealousy would surface, along with resentment that her daughter would not be able to benefit from having a *daed* of her own. Lizzie would never dream of calling him out after all this time. After all, she's the one that left and never told him where she was going. But she was just a young girl, and he'd made it plenty clear to her that he wanted nothing more to do with her. Being the coward that he was, he'd passed the message along with her older *bruder*, David. If he'd had the courage to face her, she would have told him she loved him, but it was all in the past, and she didn't intend on socializing with the community who had likely shunned her, so it wouldn't be an issue to avoid Jacob and his family.

———

Abby watched the landscaping go by from the window of the cab. She was angry with her mom, who hadn't explained much to her about why they were running away from the only life Abby had ever known. She'd treated her like a baby when she'd asked her mom questions about Eddie. Despite Lizzie's efforts to sugar-coat the truth, and let Abby think he was just an old friend who had problems, she saw right through her mom's stories to protect her from the truth. She knew there was more to the story than what she'd been told, but all she cared about was that he seemed to be the reason they left Ohio, and that didn't make any sense to her since the man was dead.

Abby didn't like feeling like her mom was lying to her. She'd overheard enough heated conversations between her mom and Eddie to know something bad was going on. During Red Ribbon week at school, Abby had learned all about the ways drugs can destroy lives, and it seemed Eddie was now a cliché of an example to her. Unfortunately, nothing in the lectures in school could have prepared her for the way that destruction would affect her own life.

Abby reached into her back pack for her cell phone; at least she could find comfort in her friends. She texted out a message to her best friend, Rachel, and then pushed send. She held her phone up hoping to get a better signal so it would send since it didn't seem to be working. She looked closely when the text failed, noting that she had several bars. She tried to resend, and became frustrated when it wouldn't work. Pushing in Rachel's number, she held it to her ear and listened to the rings until an automated message answered her call. She held the phone out to look at the face, thinking she'd punched the wrong number. Hanging up, she tried it again. The same message came up.

She pushed the phone toward Lizzie, who was lost in her own thoughts. "There's something wrong with my phone. I can't call Rachel!"

Lizzie pulled the phone to her ear and listened to the message. "I haven't paid the bill, Abby, I'm sorry."

Abby pushed the phone back toward her mother when she tried to give it back to her. "Can't you pay the bill so I can talk to Rachel? If I can't talk to her, I won't be able to get through this vacation."

Lizzie put the phone down on the seat between them and turned to her daughter. "I'll get us new phones when we settle in Indiana and I get a job. Until then, I'm afraid you're going to have to be without communication with your friends. And this isn't a vacation. We aren't going back to Ohio."

Abby snatched the phone up from the seat of the cab, and shot a look at Lizzie that alarmed her. "What do mean we aren't going back? All my friends are there! I don't want a new phone; I want you to turn this one back on so I can call Rachel. Please, Mom!"

Lizzie gazed at the prying eyes of the cab driver in the rearview mirror. "We can talk about this when we get to the Bed & Breakfast."

Abby crossed her arms in defiance. "My life is going to be ruined unless you turn my phone back on!"

Lizzie looked at her sternly. "I'm not turning it back on, so drop it, Abby."

Abby rolled down the window of the cab and tossed the phone out the window, watching it bounce along the road while the cab sped away from it. Lizzie didn't even notice; she was too wrapped up in what she was going to say to her *aenti* when they arrived at the Bed & Breakfast.

Abby turned her face back toward the window, watching the farms go by slowly. She didn't see any malls or schools, or even a McDonald's anywhere. What was she going to do so far away from everything and everyone she cared about? Her mother rattled on about how good the move would be for them, and that she had a surprise for Abby, but she didn't care. She was wearing an itchy dress that she'd surely be teased for if her friends could see her, and she couldn't see past the miles of farmland and endless ribbons of road that led her further away from her life.

CHAPTER 4

Caleb sat under a tree with a plate of fried chicken that Miriam Graber handed to him, and now she was talking his ear off about how much help he'd been all day to his *daed.* He ignored her, realizing that the sudden attention had to do with the conversations he'd overheard the women discussing that involved his *daed,* and his newly shaven face, leaving them hoping he was thinking of taking a wife. Martha Schrock was busy trying to hand him a plate piled high with cakes and pastries, asking if he would take it to his *daed,* when Caleb noticed the beardless man ducking behind a tree near the pond. He watched his *daed* for several minutes before deciding to walk down to the pond and see why he was hiding from these women who were eager to be his new *mamm.*

Caleb picked up a rock and tossed it sideways toward the pond just like Jacob had shown him the previous summer. He watched in awe as it skipped across the glassy surface several times before sinking to the bottom. "Look, *Daed,* I did it just like ya showed me!"

Jacob placed a hand on his son's shoulder, feeling a little bit of pride as he watched the rings slowly disappear on the sparkling water. He couldn't help himself when it came to Caleb, but it humbled him to know that the boy looked up to him so much. Twinges of guilt tried to ruin the moment with thoughts that Nellie would never see her son do any of the simple things that Jacob sometimes took for granted. He'd seen his son soaking up the attention of Miriam and Martha, who would each probably make fine *mamm's* for his son, and he felt selfish for denying him the one thing that was within his power to give. He would never be able to give him his real *mamm,* but he could give the boy what he craved…a new *mamm.* He'd been selfish with his son long enough and maybe it was time to revisit the idea of taking a *fraa*—for Caleb's sake.

"I saw you talking to Miss Martha and Miss Miriam. I'm guessing you think that either of them would make a fine *mamm* for you."

Jacob's heart did a summersault in his chest at the thought of it. He suddenly felt well beyond the twenty-eight years that he was. He felt he was much too young to be a widower, and considering a second marriage with a woman who would most like want her own *kind* in addition to raising Caleb. Was he ready to start all over again with a *boppli* with Caleb being ten years old? Was he really ready to marry just for the sake of giving Caleb a *mamm?* Maybe not, but perhaps it would make up for the sins of his past.

Caleb looked up at his *daed* and studied him for a moment. "I heard the women talking about the fact you shaved off your *baard*. They think you want to get married." He continued to study Jacob. "Is it true?"

Jacob took in a lung-full of fresh air and then let it out. "If you're wanting a *mamm,* I'd be willing to take it under consideration."

Caleb shook his head disappointedly. "It would be nice to have a *mamm*. And a *bruder."*

Jacob choked down his son's bold statement.

"Maybe you're putting the cart before the horse, Caleb. I haven't even asked either of them if I could call on them properly. It's a process that takes time."

He hoped the statement would satisfy the lad until he could think of a way out of the mess, but by the expression on Caleb's face, this wasn't going to be easy.

ଇଠାଓଷ

Lizzie shook as she stepped out of the cab. The driver was already at the trunk retrieving their small suitcases, but Lizzie's feet felt heavy as she heaved her backpack over her shoulder and tried to step toward the front walk of the B&B. She took note that the oversized home had been recently painted, and four freshly painted rocking chairs graced the front porch that was surrounded by flowering plants in a myriad of colors. She could hear ducks on the pond quacking happily. Oh how she'd missed that sound. And the smell of the water floating gently on the breeze. The only thing that would make this moment less stressful was a tall glass of lemonade and a trip back in time. She glanced over at Abby feeling guilty for thinking such a selfish thought. But she was nervous about being so near her *daed*—even if she wouldn't be seeing him.

Aunt Bess came running out the front door, her apron flying in the breeze as she planted herself in front of Lizzie. "*Wie gehts,* Elizabeth*?* I've missed you so much!"

Bess hugged Lizzie so hard she nearly took her breath away. Her *aenti* smelled of fresh-baked bread and smoked ham, no doubt from preparing for their visit. Lizzie felt the warmth of the older woman's embrace, feeling like she was finally home.

Aunt Bess pulled away and examined Abby. "Who is this precious *kind* with such a long face?"

"This is my *dochder,* Abby."

The word felt strange coming from Lizzie's lips, and Abby looked at her quizzically. She knew she would have a lot of explaining to do, but not yet. She wanted to settle in first, and *then* break the news to Abby that they were here for *gut*—with Lizzie's *family*e. She hoped to be able to see her *vadder* and younger *bruder,* Seth, but she was sure she had been shunned at some point over the last eleven years since she'd turned her back on Amish soil.

Her *aenti* pulled Lizzie close again and whispered in her ear. "I see by your garb that you are planning on re-joining the community, *jah?*"

Lizzie swallowed hard. "*Nee.* I made the dresses and *kapps* as a disguise. I'll explain everything later."

Aunt Bess pulled away from Lizzie, her smile unfading, and picked up their suitcases and headed inside the B&B. Lizzie looked at Abby, who was wearing a scowl deep enough to cause concern, but it wasn't something that could be helped at the moment. Lizzie wondered how long the child would remain silent, but giving her the cold shoulder for the time being was probably best until she could explain everything to her *aenti* without Abby blurting out the wrong thing.

CHAPTER 5

Jacob had managed to carefully avoid Martha and Miriam the remainder of the work day, despite their many attempts at cornering him and offering to feed him their cooking. As his neighbors left his stretch of land, he thanked *Gott* that at least Caleb had given up his quest for a new *mamm* for the time being. Tomorrow would be a new day to fight the battle, but he hoped that Caleb would be too distracted with helping the *menner* with the harvest to pester him anymore.

By the end of the week, they would be at the Beiler farm for the barn-raising, and Jacob worried that being around Jonah would only remind him of his desire for a new *familye* just like his. Jacob thought that perhaps he should consider taking in an older widow to cook and clean to give Caleb a break from his cooking, and the chore of housecleaning they shared along with the chores of running the farm. Maybe then Caleb would give up his quest for a new *mamm,* and Jacob wouldn't have to worry about becoming involved in another loveless marriage. It wasn't that Jacob was against marriage; he had never gotten over his first love and didn't want to repeat the mistake he'd made in marrying Nellie.

Jacob laid his weary head on his pillow, willing the memories of Lizzie to leave him. Why was he still thinking of her after all these years? And with his *fraa* being dead for ten years, he should be thinking of her, instead of the one that got away almost eleven years ago.

Over the years, he'd continuously thought that if he could have seen Lizzie one last time—or even been able to say goodbye, that it would be easier for him to deal with, than the reality of never seeing her again, and always wondering what had become of her. Even her own *familye* had not heard from her in the eleven years since her disappearance. Because there was no word from her, there had never been a formal shunning; the community and Jacob had feared she was dead.

ඞලൠ

Lizzie tucked Abby into the thick quilt of the room at the far end of the B&B that Aunt Bess set aside for visiting families. Lizzie didn't mind sharing the room with her daughter, but she wasn't sure Abby was too happy about it.

"How long are we staying here? Don't get me wrong—I like your Aunt Bess, but she dresses in the same strange clothes you made us wear to get here. Are you going to make me wear those clothes while we're here?"

Lizzie sighed. She knew Abby would be full of questions, but she just needed a good night's rest before she tackled her daughter's protest over their living situation and her curiosity about the family she was meeting for the first time.

"How about we take a walk down to the pond after breakfast and I'll tell you everything. But right now, I think we should get some sleep. It's been a really long day."

Abby crossed her arms and looked away. "But I don't want to have a talk tomorrow. I want to go home. I want to sleep in my own bed and watch TV. I didn't see a single TV in this house!"

Lizzie turned her daughter's chin toward her and looked her in the eye. "You know I had to sell everything to come here. And the house belongs to the landlord. I'm sorry, but you will have to get used to living here—at least until we can get our own place again. As far as TV goes, you're going to have to live without it for now. Amish don't watch TV."

"That's just wrong, Mother!"

Lizzie snuffed out the light that rested on the table between the two beds and crawled beneath the warm, homemade quilt. The bedding smelled like it had been dried outside on the clothesline in the sunshine.

Oh how Lizzie had missed that smell…

ᘒᑕᘒ

Lizzie opened her eyes at first light. She could hear the ducks quacking outside the open window. Her *aenti* was more than likely at the pond's edge with her toes dipped in the water, throwing bread to the ducks. Forcing herself from the cocoon of quilts, Lizzie followed the smell of fresh-brewed coffee to the kitchen.

Aunt Bess entered in through the back door and set an empty bread basket on the table. "I knew you'd wake up when ya smelled the *kaffi* brewing."

Lizzie smiled. "Actually it was the furiously hungry ducks that stirred me this morning, but I slept like a *boppli*. I haven't slept that soundly in some time."

Her *aenti* smiled. "Are ya ready to tell me why you're here? And without a *mann* or a *vadder* for the *kind?*"

"I don't have a husband, and her *vadder* is gone."

Aunt Bess put a hand under Lizzie's chin, forcing her to look into her eyes. "You're too young to be without a husband. There are several widowers in the community, but the only one your age is Jacob Yoder. I know the two of you were in *lieb* when you were *kinner,* perhaps you could get to know him again. He owns the farm and all the land on the other side of pond, just down the lane."

Her *aenti* pointed in the direction of his farm, but Lizzie had let her vision blur at the mention of Jacob. The thought of him married broke her heart all over again. Had he married Nellie Fisher after she left the community? She knew she had no right to be upset that Jacob had taken a *fraa,* but she'd always hoped he would marry *her* someday.

CHAPTER 6

Abby sat on the landing of the stairs listening to her mother and great aunt talk. She knew better than to eavesdrop, but the mention of the name Jacob Yoder pricked her ears. It was the name listed on her birth certificate as her father. And now Aunt Bess was saying he lived on the other side of the pond. She wondered why her mother was keeping her father from her if he was this close to them. She was certain her mother would say she had "grown-up" reasons for not telling her, but Abby didn't care—she was still mad at her mother for letting her cell phone—the only avenue to the outside world, get turned off and refusing to pay the bill.

Abby continued to listen as her great aunt explained to her mother that Jacob had been married, and how his wife had died giving birth to his son, Caleb, who was just a few months younger than

Abby. Was it possible that Caleb was her brother? Did she even want a brother? A sister most certainly, but a brother?

Abby went back upstairs, determined to pack her small suitcase and leave this backward home. Her mother had lied to her about a lot of things, and she was now more angry than ever. She didn't want to be Amish for a single minute longer. She was certain that her brother had a TV, and probably video games. But most of all, she hoped her dad would have a cell phone she could use to call Rachel.

&ⵘ

Abby had managed to slip out the front door of the B&B without her mother or great aunt noticing her. Aunt Bess was in the middle of offering her mother a job to clean the upstairs rooms of the B&B since the older woman suffered from swollen knees and it hurt her back to climb the stairs and stoop to clean. Her mother eagerly accepted, leaving Abby as the last one to be informed she was planning on staying in the area for an extended period of time, which only added fuel to Abby's already full plate of anger for her mother at the present time.

Pulling on her straw hat to shield her eyes from the sun, Abby walked slowly down the long, country road to the other side of the pond, where she was certain life would be much easier for her.

&ⵘ

Caleb scattered feed for the chickens as he watched the barefoot *Englischer* walk down the lane toward their farm. Who was she, and why was she walking toward him with a funny look on her face? He watched with a laugh in his heart when she struggled to keep the oversized straw hat from blowing off her head in the breeze. She seemed to look lost as she looked around her, and then set her eyes back on Caleb. Walking up the long path toward his home, he noticed a sense of determination in her that he'd never seen before. She didn't look much older than he was, but the suitcase she toted carelessly at her side suggested she thought she was old enough to be on her own.

As she approached Caleb, she examined him from head to toe, and then let her eyes wander to the surrounding farm.

Caleb stepped in her path. "Are you lost or running away?"

Abby stopped scanning the property and set her eyes on Caleb. "Both. Do you know where I can find Jacob Yoder?"

Caleb pointed behind him. "He's in the barn. What do ya want with him?"

Abby set her jaw upward. "That's private."

Caleb watched the girl walk toward the barn and disappear in the shadow of the open doorway.

ՑՄՅ

Abby walked cautiously toward the barn and entered through the open door. She hoped she wasn't in the wrong place, assuming the young farm-hand had steered her in the right direction. As she approached a man mucking out one of the horse stalls, she examined him from the short distance that separated them. On his head was a straw hat like the young boy was wearing, and his clothing was the same style, but he didn't have the beard she'd witnessed the Amish men his age wearing when she and her mother rode through town yesterday in their cab ride to the B&B.

Taking a brave step forward, Abby cleared her throat to get the man's attention. He looked up and leaned against his pitchfork. "Excuse me, Sir. Can you tell me where I can find Jacob Yoder?"

Jacob stepped out of the stall and set aside the pitch fork to close part of the distance between them. "I am Jacob Yoder. Who might you be?"

Jacob took another step forward.

"I'm Lizzie's daughter."

Jacob pulled of his hat and blew out a heavy sigh.

"Lizzie Miller?"

Abby set her suitcase down and moved toward the horse that seemed anxious for her attention. "That was her name when she was younger, but she changed it when she left home. At least that what she told me, but she's been keeping some secrets from me my whole life that I'm just now finding out—like where my father was all this time."

Jacob looked into the girl's eyes. He could see Lizzie in them, and it scared him that she could look just like her mother did when they had attended school together.

"I'm not sure how I can help you. What is your name?"

Abby reached up and touched the horse nickering for attention on his soft nose. "My name is Abby, and my birth certificate says Jacob Yoder is my father. When I heard my mom and Aunt Bess talking this morning about you living here, I decided to come here and let you be a father to me. I'm mad at her for lying to me, and I don't want to go back there. She is expecting me to be Amish just because she is." Abby fanned out the skirt of her white sundress. "I like wearing my own dresses, not the itchy Amish ones that she made us wear when we came here so Eddie's thugs wouldn't find us."

Jacob looked behind him at the milking stool and collapsed onto it before he lost his balance. He knew he hadn't fathered Lizzie's child since they had never been intimate, but he wondered why she would name him as father on the girl's birth certificate. He couldn't think straight. "Who is Eddie? And why are his *thugs* looking for you? Are you and your *mamm* in some sort of danger?"

Abby continued to stroke the horse on the nose.

"Eddie is this mean guy that used to come over and hit my mom and make her give him money, but he's dead now. He crashed mom's car. But now his thugs came over and told mom to give them the money Eddie owed them. That's why we dressed in the Amish clothes to come here and hide from those men. They had a gun."

Jacob took in a deep breath, trying to digest the little girl's ramblings. He wasn't so sheltered that he didn't know what the word *thug* meant. He also knew the danger of having unsavory characters looking for Lizzie and this child—the child who seemed to think he was her *daed*.

CHAPTER 7

Bess poured a third cup of coffee, emptying the pot. "Should I brew another pot of *kaffi?*"

Lizzie shook her head. "I'm good. If I drink any more I won't sleep later."

Bess sat down across from Lizzie and stared into her cup. "Do ya plan on going home, Elizabeth?"

"Do ya mean to see my *daed* and *bruder?*"

"*Jah.* You haven't been shunned. It's not too late."

Lizzie stood and began to pace the small kitchen, despite her *aenti's* prodding to sit back down. "Ya don't understand. I won't be welcomed back into the community. Mine would be considered the longest running *rumspringa* in the history of this community. Besides, you're forgetting I had a child out of wedlock."

Bess stood beside her and placed loving arms around her. "If ya confess all that to the Bishop, he will baptize you. *Gott* himself doesn't hold that against you; how can the elders hold it against you that Eddie drugged you and compromised you? And now he's *dot,* so in the eyes of the elders, they may consider you a widow."

Lizzie sighed. "I think you're giving them more credit than what they're due. The elders and the Bishop will not be so quick to overlook my transgressions."

"Then give a general confession, and the rest will be our little secret—and between you and *Gott,* of course."

Lizzie hugged her *aenti,* grateful for her discretion. But there was just a little bit more to her story that she needed to reveal.

"When I found out I was pregnant, I moved to a small, unincorporated community in Ohio named Barlow. I chose the community because it reminded me a little of the Amish community. Once I settled in, I legally changed my name to Lizzie Barlow."

Bess crinkled her brow. "What was the significance of the name?"

"I chose the name Lizzie because that's what Jacob always called me, and I was still very much in love with him at the time."

The confession brought tears to Lizzie's eyes. Though the mere thought of Jacob filled her with regret, she knew if she hadn't left, she wouldn't have Abby. Besides, she would never have been able to bear watching Jacob court and marry Nellie Fisher if she'd stayed. Her life had not been easy since she left home, but maybe that was all about to change.

ಬಿಲ್ಲ

Jacob stood on wobbly legs. He had no idea how he would explain to this child he wasn't her father, but the worry on the forefront was Lizzie. He was already way behind in his chores, and would need to complete them before he could take Abby back. It didn't seem likely that he would be able to convince her to go back on her own, and he worried that Lizzie would be frantic over her disappearance—especially given the story that she'd relayed to him about the danger they may be in. But the truth of the matter was that he didn't have a phone to call her at the B&B, and a small part of him hoped Lizzie herself would show up on his property to claim her *dochder*. Though he was eager to see her again, he was more than a little disturbed by Lizzie's actions. They had put him in quite the predicament.

Jacob faced Abby and cleared his throat as if the act could somehow give him the words to say to her. "My son Caleb is in the yard feeding the chickens, but I can assume he's moved on to the pigs by this time. Would you like to go out and help him so I can get a few things finished here, and then we can sit in the house and maybe have some lunch before we go have a talk with your *mamm*—I mean your mom?"

Abby took a small leap backward and squealed, leaving Jacob searching for a snake or a spider. "I don't want to go back. She's trying to make me Amish and I don't like it."

Jacob chuckled. "I'm Amish, Abby."

Abby's eyes filled with tears. "Then it's true. I'm Amish and there's nothing I can do about it."

"Being Amish is a very *gut* thing, not a bad thing. Didn't your *madder* tell you that?"

"You mean my *mother?*"

Jacob nodded.

"She never told me we were Amish before yesterday. And she didn't tell me anything about *you*. When I saw my birth certificate, I asked her about the name, and she just said that was the name of my real father. Every time I tried to ask her anything about you, she would turn all sad, and sometimes she'd cry. So I stopped asking her."

Jacob's heart sank. How could he tell Abby the truth when she'd been told he was her *vadder?* This was Lizzie's mess, and she would have to be the one to get herself out of it.

Abby looked up at Jacob, tears streaming down her face. "How come you never came looking for me?"

Jacob searched for the right words. "I'm sorry you're upset Abby, but I didn't know anything about you either until you showed up here on my farm."

Abby cried harder. "But you're my father, you should have known about me!"

Jacob looked up when movement in the doorway caught his eye. Caleb entered the barn, and circled Abby.

"Is she my *schweschder?*"

Jacob stood between them. "This is not your business, Caleb."

He ignored his father. "Is your *mamm dot* too?"

Abby crossed her arms. "Will you guys speak English around me, cuz I don't understand your language."

Jacob felt distraught over Abby's lack of knowledge of her heritage. "Didn't your *mamm* teach you the Amish language?"

"I already told you. She told me yesterday she was Amish, and that I am too. She's never talked like that, but I heard her say some funny words to her Aunt Bess."

"My son wanted to know if your mom was still alive."

Abby turned to Caleb. "She's very much alive. Why would you ask me such a thing?"

Caleb's gaze fell to the ground. "Because my *mamm* is not. She died when she was birthing me."

Abby gulped.

Caleb looked at his *daed* with hopeful eyes. "If she's my *schweschder,* does that mean her *mamm* will want to be my new *mamm?*"

Jacob looked at his son sternly. "*Halten* Caleb."

Abby's eyes grew wide. "He wants my mom to be *his* mom?"

Jacob ignored her question. "Caleb, take Abby into the *haus* and get her some lemonade, and then get back to your chores. When I finish in the barn, I'll hitch up the buggy, and we will take you back so I can have a grownup talk with your mom."

Both children obeyed Jacob's orders, and skipped up to the house, leaving him with a lot of conflicting thoughts.

CHAPTER 8

Lizzie yawned and leaned back in her chair to get a better look at the kitchen clock. "I should go check on Abby. If I let her sleep any longer, she'll be wired the rest of the day. And I won't be able to get her to sit still long enough to talk to her about everything."

Dragging her feet up the stairs, Lizzie felt the weight of her day already slowing her down. She was not looking forward to having to explain everything to her daughter, who was already starting to rebel against her. If she wasn't careful, she would drive her child away even further, but if she continued to sugar-coat the truth, she would never have her daughter's respect.

Lizzie opened the door to the room they shared and noticed Abby's bed was empty. Scanning the room, she immediately noticed Abby's small suitcase was no longer on the floor in a disheveled mess where she'd left it. Knowing she'd warned her daughter to put it away in the morning or forfeit her breakfast, she peeked into the closet to see if it was tossed carelessly in there or if she'd closed it and put it away neatly like she was asked to do. Alarmed by the empty space were her daughter's suitcase should be, Lizzie's heart skipped a beat. Immediately dropping to the floor, she pulled up the dust-ruffle to search for it under the bed.

It wasn't there.

Lizzie threw back the covers of Abby's bed, but still, nothing.

There was no trace of Abby left in the room.

Lizzie's heart slammed against her ribcage as she practically flew down the stairs to the kitchen. Out of breath, she found her *aenti* still sitting at the table savoring her last cup of *kaffi*.

"Abby's gone!"

Bess pushed the chair behind her, stepping forward to steady Lizzie. "Sit down and take a deep breath and define *gone.*"

Lizzie allowed the woman to guide her into the chair she'd been comfortable in just moments ago. "She's not upstairs. Her suitcase is gone. We *have* to go look for her."

Bess straightened her apron and held a hand across her ample breast. "She's on foot, so she couldn't have gotten far. Let me call the surrounding people with phones in their barns and ask them to start searching for her. Your *daed* is the furthest out on the main road…is it okay if I call him?"

Lizzie didn't have to think about it. "Yes! Call him—but don't tell him details—only that the daughter of a guest is missing—please, *aenti*—I don't want him to find out about his *kinskind* in this way."

Bess nodded while Lizzie ran out to the barn to begin hitching the horse to her *aenti's* buggy. She was confident she remembered how to hitch up a horse, but more than that, she needed something to keep her hands busy while Aunt Bess made the phone calls. She wouldn't allow herself to think beyond her daughter's obvious reasons for running off. She'd lied to her about a lot of things, and she understood the child's tantrum. But with danger lurking over their heads because of Eddie, she feared for her daughter's safety more than ever. Trying desperately to think logically, she knew they had gotten far enough away, and in a remote enough place that it was highly unlikely that the thugs would be able to track her down, but she knew that even as cautious as she was about leaving no trail, they could still find her.

Grateful that the gelding was patient with her nervous fumbling of the harnesses, Lizzie was able to hitch the horse fairly quickly. Just as she finished, her *aenti* was out the door, draping a shawl over her shoulders, and hoisting herself into the buggy. Lizzie climbed up beside her and took the reins, and slapped them gently against the gelding.

ଈଓଔଷ

Jacob worked quickly, knowing that every minute that Abby remained on his farm was another minute that Lizzie would be worried about her *dochder.* Unfortunately, it just couldn't be helped. He had a cow to milk and animals to feed before he could take her back. The rest of his chores could wait until later, but the animals couldn't wait for their grain.

His mind drifted to his younger days when he was courting Lizzie. He remembered how angry and hurt he was that she'd sent her eldest *bruder,* David, to break off their relationship as if it had meant nothing to her. He'd intended to marry her—to have a *familye* with her, and grow old with her. And now she comes back to the community with another man's *kind,* trying to claim he'd fathered her. He would be excommunicated from the community if the elders were to discover this, and it would ruin his reputation as a trusted member of the community.

A small part of him wanted to hold onto the memory of Lizzie when she was young and innocent of the ways of the *Englischers,* but that was next to impossible with evidence to the contrary that had invaded his own home.

ജ෬

In the house, Abby was amazed by the things Caleb continued to point out that *their* dad had made. Every piece of furniture was carved to perfection. And the solid wood banister on the stairway tempted Abby to slide down it. It was a fine house indeed, and Abby hadn't even noticed the lack of televisions or other electronic equipment.

The "tour" was contained to the downstairs rooms, but Abby's favorite room was a sun porch with a fireplace and two cozy rocking chairs. Her mom used to rock her when she was younger, but they had been forced to part with the one piece of furniture with any sentimental value when her mother decided to move them here. A renewed sense of anger welled up in Abby, but she quickly pushed it aside, realizing she was beginning to miss her mom.

❧❧❧

Lizzie steered the gelding toward the main road, lost in her thoughts. Too many emotions attacked her at the moment, and she feared she would not be able to contain her composure much longer. She chided herself for thinking that coming to the Amish community would solve her problems. But running away seemed to be what she did best. And now, it seemed, she'd passed that trait onto her only child. Abby had left willingly—packed her suitcase and left. She wondered if this is how her *daed* had felt when she ran away from home nearly eleven years ago. Lizzie feared for Abby, who was much younger than she had been when she left. She wasn't capable of taking care of herself in dangerous situations. Although, to be honest, she hadn't been either, or she wouldn't even have had Abby in the first place.

Lizzie pushed aside thoughts of the past. She had to find her daughter, and even the fear of seeing her *daed* and *brieder* for the first time in eleven years couldn't compare to the fear she held for her *boppli*.

CHAPTER 9

Lizzie wrung her hands while her *aenti* prepared *kaffi* and sliced cake for the neighbors who had already arrived back at the B&B empty-handed. Though the original plan was for everyone to meet back at the B&B at noon whether they'd found her or not, Lizzie wasn't certain she could wait even another minute.

"We have to call the police, Aunt Bess!"

Bess steered her to an empty chair. "You know better than anyone that the police will not consider her missing for another few hours. And we still have people out looking. There are three, including your *daed* who have not yet reported back here. We'll wait a few more minutes on them before we make the call. It's nearly noon. I know it's tough, but give it until your *daed* arrives."

Tears welled up in Lizzie's eyes threatening to spill over, but she swallowed them down, determined to brave this out for Abby's sake. She offered up a plea to *Gott,* asking for forgiveness for her past mistakes, asking that He not hold it against Abby for the way she came into this world. Guilt consumed her, despite every effort to let *Gott* heal her of her past transgressions. At the moment, she didn't feel very forgivable.

⁎⁎⁎

Jacob assisted Abby onto the front bench of the buggy alongside him and Caleb. The *kind* was fascinated by the mode of transportation, exclaiming she felt like she'd stepped into the pages of a fairytale. He imagined what it would be like to be Abby's *daed.* He'd wanted a *dochder,* but he never got that opportunity since his *fraa* died. The fact remained; Abby was not his *kind,* and he needed to return her to Lizzie. The very thought of Lizzie heated his face. Was it possible he still had feelings for her?

⁎⁎⁎

Hiram Miller pulled into the yard of the B&B, his *buwe,* Seth seated next to him. Seth jumped from the buggy the moment he saw Lizzie and ran to her, pulling her into his arms.

"We thought you were *dot.*"

Lizzie wriggled from his strong arms. "I'm still very much alive! You're all grown up, little *bruder.*"

He ruffled Lizzie's hair. "I'm taller than you are now, so you can't tease me anymore."

Lizzie smiled at her younger sibling until her *daed* stepped into her line of vision, a stern look on his face.

"Does your presence here mean you've finally put your *rumspringa* behind you, and you're ready to fully embrace our faith?"

Lizzie lowered her gaze in respect. "*Jah.*"

"*Das gut.* When we find the missing *kind* I will fetch the Bishop and we will get you baptized at once."

Lizzie kept her eyes downcast. "*Daed,* the missing *kind* is my *dochder* and she's your *kinskind.*"

Before he could say a word, another buggy pulled into the yard and Abby jumped out, rushing to Lizzie's side. "I'm so sorry, Mom. I didn't mean to run off. But I found my dad!"

No sooner had she said it, than a handsome man with familiar, blue-green eyes stood before them holding Abby's suitcase out to her. She looked at the boy-turned-man, the very one she used to love. The boyish glint in his eyes was replaced by small crow's feet in the corners. The sides of his sandy brown hair were peppered with a little gray. But his chin was clean-shaven. If it was possible, he was even more handsome than she'd thought when they were teenagers. He was no longer a skinny teenager, but a well-built man who still made her heart flutter.

Abby slipped her hand in Jacob's. "See Mom, I found my father."

Lizzie looked into Jacob's face, her heart slamming against her chest wall at her daughter's blunt words.

Hiram Miller pushed between them. "Is this true, Jacob? Did you *vadder* this *kind?"*

Jacob swallowed. "Maybe we should all go inside and have a talk about this."

Hiram pursed his lips. "There is nothing to talk about. Seth, go fetch the Bishop. Tell him we will be needing him for a confession and a *hochzich.* Elizabeth, you get into a blue dress, and get out of those *Englisch* clothes at once."

Lizzie stomped her foot. *"Daed,* you can't make me marry this man! I don't even know him anymore."

Hiram narrowed his eyes at Lizzie. "You knew him well enough to have a *boppli.* I knew I should have taken sooner measures to separate the two of you instead waiting like a fool, thinking I could trust either of you."

His harsh words rang in Lizzie's and Jacob's ears, causing them to look at one another with grief.

*"Ach, y*ou're the one that broke us apart all those years ago? David told me Lizzie—Elizabeth— didn't wish to see me anymore."

The sound of her name on Jacob's lips sent a wave of heat through her belly. He was the only one that had called her Lizzie. What once had been a term of endearment had become her permanent legal name.

And now her father was ruining every memory she had of Jacob and trying to force them to marry over a mistake she had made in placing Jacob's name on Abby's birth certificate as a measure to keep her safe from Eddie.

"*Daed,* did you tell my *bruder* to lie to me about Jacob not wanting to see me anymore?"

Hiram narrowed his eyes. "I was doing what was best for you, but it seems that you allowed Jacob to disgrace you and compromise you before I could end it."

"But I didn't..."

"Silence *dochder.* If you want to remain in this community you will marry Jacob and make this right. "

Hiram turned to Jacob, who was looking into the hopeful eyes of his own son. "What have you to say for your actions? To *vadder* two *kinner* so close in age—it's disgraceful. And marrying another after the way you behaved with my *dochder.* You should have married my *dochder,* but instead you married poor Nellie Fisher and planted your seed with her too! Have you no shame?"

As shocked as he was by Hiram Miller's accusations, Jacob knew that to deny the claim would be to risk being shunned, especially if his name really was on the child's birth certificate. The community would have no reason to doubt Lizzie's word or her honor. Yes, an admission would be a way to give Caleb the new *mamm* that he desired, but above all, he didn't want to be the reason Lizzie left the community a second time since they'd not had any closure the first time. And here she was standing before him now, looking more lovely than he ever imagined.

"Forgive me, Hiram. I will marry Elizabeth and make this right."

Lizzie couldn't believe what she was hearing. "But Jacob, you can't…"

Hiram stepped between them. "When Seth returns with the Bishop we will have *two* confessions and a wedding."

Lizzie couldn't look at Jacob. She was so embarrassed. Abby clung to her side, and Caleb stepped forward and slipped his hand in hers.

"I'm Caleb. I'm *froh* you will be my new *mamm.*"

His statement nearly broke her heart, and from the look on Jacob's downcast face, it had affected him the same way. Lizzie couldn't help but smile back at Caleb, his innocent eyes gleaming.

CHAPTER 10

Lizzie had very little recollection of what happened for the next few hours while she was coerced into a confession, baptized, and finally married. Thankfully, she'd remembered her *aenti's* advice regarding a general confession. She knew that the way Abby was brought into this world was against the ways of the people, and *Gott's* word, so she felt relief that she was finally rid of the burden she'd carried for the past eleven years. Abby had given her a little grief when she was dressing in the blue dress that her *aenti* had loaned her, but she quickly calmed down when she realized she would finally have the dad she had wanted her entire ten years.

Before Lizzie realized, her *daed* and *aenti* were hugging her and welcoming her back into the community. She couldn't help but weep happy tears that her *daed* and *brieder* were back in her life. And she had a husband, which would finally allow her to hold her head up. But her heart quickened at the thought of being married to a man she once loved as a young girl, but who was now a stranger to her in every way. Even at their ceremony there was no exchange of a kiss between them. She knew she could learn to love him again; she already respected him for not shaming her in front of her family, and was grateful he'd taken the blame away from her. She would have a lifetime with him to try to make up for the position she'd put him in, and hoped he would eventually forgive her.

›‹

  Jacob watched Lizzie as she pasted on a smile from ear to ear while her *familye* welcomed her back into the community, and he told himself he'd done the right thing. For him, Caleb, and for Lizzie and Abby. Having a *fraa* would be good for him. He had to admit that he was nervous about her expectations, and wasn't sure he was immediately ready to fulfill any obligations other than provider. It would take him a while to let go of the irritation he felt over being forced into a marriage that he would have preferred to decide for himself. She was beautiful, and he was certainly attracted to her, but she had been living among the *Englisch* for the past ten-plus years, and he had no idea what kind of person she'd become. Only the fact that she'd accepted the baptism, had he felt comfortable enough to have her as his son's *mamm.*

He continued to watch her as she made her way through the friends and family that had been present after arriving for the earlier search of Abby. Since they had remained for the wedding, he felt obligated to greet them and accept their well-wishes along-side his *fraa,* but he couldn't help but be mesmerized by this woman who was now his *fraa,* and yet a stranger in every way.

୫୬୯

Caleb led Abby out to the barn to play with the kittens that Aunt Bess had told them about. Abby was unsure of her new role as big sister, and wasn't sure she could get used to the way they talked. But she was happiest about having a new dad, and a little brother was a small price to pay for that. She only hoped he wasn't whiny or needy the way her friend's siblings had been when she visited them.

"Is your *aenti* going to let us take one of the kittens home with us?"

"What do you mean *home?* I live here now."

"You will move into our *haus* now since your *mamm* married my *daed*—our *daed.*"

"I don't think we're moving in your house."

"When my friend's *daed* married his new *mamm,* she moved in their house with them."

"If I move in with you do I get my own horse?"

"If you ask *daed* he will get you one. I have my own horse, and chickens, and a milking cow."

"I don't want any of that—just a horse. And one of these cute little kittens."

Caleb picked up a black kitten with white paws. "I want this one."

Abby snuggled up to two of them who purred and nuzzled her neck. "I want them all."

"We might be able to convince *daed* to let us each have one if we tell him they'll be good mousers."

"No! I don't want them catching mice. That's terrible and I won't let my kitten kill cute little mice."

"*Daed* will be more agreeable if we tell him we want them to catch the mice in the barn. They can become a problem when they get into the sacks of grain we use to feed the animals."

"I guess you're right, but I don't like the idea of it. Do you really think mom and dad will let us keep them?"

Caleb chuckled. "All we have to do is put on our sad face and *daed* will give in."

Caleb demonstrated his best sad face, and the two of them giggled. Abby thought that maybe having a little brother wouldn't be so bad after all.

❧

Lizzie was so happy to be back with her *daed* and her younger *bruder,* Seth, that she had let go of the anger she had felt before the wedding. She would have to find a way to put aside the past, and move beyond the fact that her *daed* and *bruder,* David had been the reason she and Jacob had been torn apart all those years ago. And though it still pricked her conscious, she reminded herself she would not have Abby if not for her family's actions.

Now, she would have to adjust to raising Nellie's child as well as her own, and she would do her best to honor her deceased *freinden* by raising her son with the same love she showed her own *dochder*.

Seth approached Lizzie as Abby wandered into the yard toting a rambunctious kitten in her arms. He knelt down beside her. "I'm your *Onkel* Seth."

Abby searched his smile for a moment, and then leaned in to whisper in his ear. "Then will you help me convince my mom to let me have this kitten to take to our new house?"

Seth winked at Abby. "I'll try, but my *schweschder*—sister can be pretty stubborn. But for my new niece, I will try my best." He patted Abby's head that had been neatly tucked under a prayer *kapp,* and stood to meet Lizzie's scrutiny.

Lizzie whispered to Seth. "I should probably ask Jacob before I give her an answer. He's my husband now."

Seth nodded before giving her a hug. "I'm *froh* you are home again. You will see, this will be a *gut* life for you."

Lizzie knew he was right. So why did she feel such a nervous feeling in her gut? For one thing, she wasn't sure how the sleeping arrangements would work in Jacob's home, and she wondered what Jacob would expect of her tonight as far as wifely duties.

CHAPTER 11

"But I don't like this room, mom! I miss my Hello Kitty posters and my stuffed animals. Can I at least get a new bedspread? This old quilt looks itchy."

Lizzie tried to be patient with her *dochder,* but her tantrums would not fare well with her new husband. He would expect order and harmony under his roof, and it was up to Lizzie to rear Abby in the humble ways of the Amish, and to help rid her of her pride. She'd tried to raise her with the basic values she was instilled with, but she had to admit that raising her *Englisch* had spoiled her.

"This is a nice room, Abby. I'm counting on you to accept this room as it is. And tomorrow we will begin to make you a few new dresses. You cannot wear your jeans or shorts anymore."

"If I'd known having a new dad would be so tough I would have kept my mouth shut. It's my fault your dad made you marry him, isn't it?"

Lizzie couldn't lay such a burden on her *dochder*. It was her own fault. Her deception had caused the chain of events that forced her into a marriage with Jacob.

"Of course it's not your fault. The decision for us to be a family was a good one. It will be good for us, you'll see."

Abby stifled a yawn. "Why was your dad so angry with you?"

"Because I hadn't been a good daughter. Because I ran away like you did today. I never told him he had a granddaughter and that was wrong for me to keep you apart from my family. And I'm so happy you're back safe and sound."

Lizzie stroked the purring kitten's fur that was curled up on Abby's bed. "Get some rest. Soon it will be morning, and you have a lot to learn about being part of an Amish family."

Abby folded her arms. "That sounds like you're gonna give me chores. Caleb told me you would."

"It won't be much different from the cooking and cleaning I've already taught you—except it will be done without the use of some of the modern conveniences we're used to, so it takes a little longer."

Abby turned her back. "That sounds like chores to me."

Lizzie bent down and kissed her *dochder* and tucked the quilt around her. After putting out the lamp at her bedside table, she closed the door gently behind her, believing she could already hear Abby snoring lightly. It had been a long day for all of them.

ಬಿಂಬ

Jacob finished nighttime prayers with Caleb, wondering if he should have included Abby. But knowing there would be plenty of time for that once she became better acquainted with the schedule he and Caleb were already used to, it would get easier to incorporate time with his new *dochder*. He didn't want to exclude her, but he didn't want to push Amish ways on her too quickly for fear she would rebel, and that could be cause for discord in the house— something he'd like to keep under control.

As he left Caleb's room, he could hear Lizzie conversing quietly with Abby and decided to go to his own room and clear out some space for his new *fraa*. He felt suddenly strange at the thought of sharing his marriage bed with another woman, and wondered how Lizzie would react.

A gentle knock at the door startled him. When he opened the door, Lizzie stood with downcast eyes, her hands twisting the corner of her apron. Jacob's thoughts flashed to a time when he had no trouble pulling her into his arms, but those days had passed, and now he felt unsure of himself.

"*Kume.* This is to be your room too. I made some room in the bureau for your things, and there is a separate set of pegs on the far wall where you can hang your dresses and aprons." Jacob pointed, but Lizzie didn't follow his hand gesture—her eyes remained downcast, and she hadn't even stepped one foot inside the room. Part of him felt sorry for her, but the other part of him was still irritated about being forced into a marriage with her before he was ready make that decision for himself. He would have to put it behind him if he was to keep peace under his roof.

"I can give you some privacy while you ready yourself for the night. I think I'd like a fresh glass of milk and another piece of the cake your *aenti* sent home with us. Would you like some too? I can bring it up here on a tray if you'd like."

Lizzie shook her head, but didn't say a word. She was already nervous enough without trying to eat something this late at night. A blush rose to her face as he brushed by her to get through the door. Knowing she didn't have much time before he would return, she closed the door after he walked toward the stairs, and picked up her suitcase from the floor and placed it on the bed. As she pushed open the lid and rifled through her things, she realized she had nothing that was considered proper to sleep in. The only thing she had was a summer nightie that would be considered immodest by her new husband. Spotting a plaid robe on Jacob's row of pegs across the room, she knew she would be able to pass for proper attire if she wore the robe over her nightgown. The last thing she wanted to do was to begin her new marriage with a lack of propriety. The least she felt she could do for Jacob after he rescued her from shame, would be to honor him in every way. Not only had he married her despite a misunderstanding, but he was giving her and her *dochder* a roof over their heads, and had agreed to take on the role of *vadder* to Abby though he wasn't even her real *vadder*.

CHAPTER 12

Jacob lifted his knuckles to the door and knocked lightly. He felt funny knocking on his own bedroom door, but he wanted to be considerate of his new bride. When he didn't hear a response, he entered the room cautiously, relieved to see Lizzie standing at the window, unaware he'd stepped inside. As he closed the door, he cleared his throat discretely, but was unable to prevent Lizzie from being startled by his sudden presence. Immediately he noticed she was wearing his robe, even though the lamp had been turned down and he could only see her by the pale moonlight entering through the sheer curtain on the window.

He pointed to the bed. "Are you ready to turn in?"

She looked toward the bed, avoiding eye-contact with him. "Honestly, I don't mean any disrespect, but I don't feel comfortable sleeping in the same bed you slept in with your previous *fraa*. I don't mind sleeping on the floor if you have extra quilts."

Jacob gathered the quilts and pillows from the bed. "I understand. I didn't have time to take care of it given the urgency of our wedding, but I will go into to town tomorrow and purchase a new bed."

Lizzie kept her head down while she took the offered bedding. "Thank you, Jacob. Perhaps when you return we can sit down and talk a little. I *am* very sorry for the predicament I placed you in."

Jacob put up a hand to stop her. "We will have plenty of time to discuss things later. I suggest we get some sleep. The sun comes up mighty early and there is much to be done."

Jacob left the room, and she could hear him opening a door down the hall as she arranged the bedding on the floor at the foot of the bed near the bureau. Just as she rested her head on the feather pillow, Jacob entered the room with two more quilts and a pillow. He let them drop to the floor near Lizzie and knelt down to prepare a bed for himself next to her.

Lizzie popped her head up off her pillow and looked him in the eye for the first time since earlier that afternoon before he'd agreed to marry her at her *daed's* insistence. "What are you doing? I agreed to sleep on the floor. You are welcome to sleep on the bed. There is no reason we should both sleep on the floor."

Jacob finished spreading out the quilts and lay down next to her. "I can't sleep in the bed if you are sleeping on the floor. It would not be honorable of me. You are my *fraa*, and I will sleep here with you until I can purchase a marriage bed that is new to both of us."

Lizzie pursed her lips, not knowing whether to be irritated with the man, or to fall in love with him all over again for being such a gentleman. But since he had placed his quilts nearly two feet from hers, and had bundled himself in a separate quilt, she could assume with great relief that nothing was expected of her tonight. Feeling anxious over when or if they would consummate their marriage Lizzie was irritated for a whole new reason. How was she ever to get any sleep between the uncomfortable floor that already hurt her back, and the uncomfortable silence that had fallen between her and her new husband?

ജ ഇ

Lizzie woke to the sound of a rooster crowing, and lingered in the quilts just for a moment before opening her eyes. If she concentrated hard enough she could trick herself into believing she was a young girl again back on her *daed's* farm, and the nightmare of having to marry Jacob had not taken place. She opened her eyes to reality, and her back felt the strain of sleeping on the hardwood floor. She turned over slowly, her back cracking a little. Neither Jacob, nor his quilts rested beside her any longer. Her head shot up, knowing he would expect a meal after his morning chores, and she wasn't ready to disappoint the man so soon.

After throwing on the work dress that her *aenti* had given her that no longer fit the aging woman, she neatly folded the quilts and placed them on the end of the bed, and then went down the hall to wake up Abby. She feared it would be a struggle to get her *dochder* out of bed and into the dress she'd made for her, but she was prepared to do battle with her for the sake of keeping her vows to Jacob in being his helpmate. She would have to curtail Abby's outspoken nature in order that she not become a bad influence on Caleb. She knew she had been too liberal with Abby, and she would not be immediately open to change.

Lizzie knocked on Abby's door before entering, but to her surprise, she was already awake. "I'm so glad you're up. That makes my job a little easier this morning."

Abby yawned. "I might be awake, but I'm not ready to get up. It wasn't such a good idea to let my kitten sleep with me. He kept me awake by pawing at my hair most of the night. And now I'm too tired to get up. Can't you take the kitten and feed him for me and let me sleep a little longer? The sun is barely up."

Lizzie pulled the quilt from Abby. "No ma'am. You need to feed him yourself. You're the one that wanted the responsibility of the kitten, so you will be the one to feed him. Maybe we can make a little bed on the floor for him tonight so you can get some sleep."

"Do I have to wear that dumb dress, or can I wear my jeans?"

Lizzie pulled the dress off the hook and handed it to Abby. "We already discussed this. I know this is a lot of change in just a few days, but you will get used to it. Hurry up and dress, I'm sure Caleb could use some help feeding the chickens."

Abby folded her arms. "You said I had to feed Mr. Whiskers. You didn't say anything about having to feed chickens too!"

Lizzie ran her hand down the kitten's back. "Is that what you've named him?"

Abby grinned. "I think it's a good name since he has such long white whiskers."

Lizzie giggled at the kitten. "He does need to grow into those whiskers!"

Abby pulled the quilt back over her. "Just five more minutes to play with Mr. Whiskers, please? Then I'll help Caleb with whatever you want."

Lizzie couldn't deny her *dochder* another few minutes of play-time with her new kitten. Especially after she'd agreed to help her new *bruder* as soon as she got up. Lizzie had already put her through so much in the last two days, she was happy Abby was being as agreeable as she was—but she was certain her mood was up only because of the kitten. And Lizzie was prepared to use it as long as it would last.

CHAPTER 13

Jacob yawned and stretched his aching back from sleeping on the floor. After getting very little sleep, he decided to get up and get an early start to his day so he could make time to go into town and purchase a new mattress for his bed so he and Lizzie would be able to sleep comfortably. But it wasn't just the hardwood floor against his back that had kept him awake. He'd wanted to pull Lizzie into his arms and hold her. Sleeping so close to her had stirred feelings in him that he thought to be long-since gone along with his youth. He'd watched her sleep for most of the night; he was in awe of her beauty, and felt disbelief that she was his *fraa.*

When he finished with the animals, he went for the long-handled razor out of habit, but decided to shave anyway. He knew that he was married now, and would be expected to grow the beard. But he and

Lizzie had not had a proper courting period, and he wanted to remain clean shaven until they consummated the marriage. The very thought of it brought heat to his face, and caused his heart to pound heavily in his chest.

He allowed the razor to glide down his chiseled jawline. Not paying any attention to what he was doing, he nicked his jaw. Too distracted to care that he was bleeding, he let his thoughts drift back to Lizzie as he continued to shave. Another nick to the other side didn't bring him from his stupor. He hadn't thought about how he was going to feel with her in his house. Wasn't this what he'd wanted since his youth? He'd let his thoughts be consumed with her to the point of confession to the Bishop just after his Nellie had passed. Though he hadn't confessed the entire truth, the guilt that he felt for not giving himself fully to the woman he'd married was his disgrace—the disgrace that would cause him to grieve for his *fraa* well beyond the normal mourning period. It's what had closed him off from the idea of marrying again. But here he was, married to the one woman who had claimed his heart so many years ago, and it frightened him beyond anything he could imagine.

ಬಿಸಿಐ

Lizzie set aside the blueberry muffins she'd baked from dried blueberries she'd found in the pantry. While they cooled, she drained the last of the bacon from the pan and scooped the scrambled eggs from the larger skillet. She was grateful that Jacob had installed a gas stove in his home, making food preparation easier for her. She would have struggled to prepare food on a wood-burning stove like she'd grown up using. As a young girl, she'd burned a lot of things before getting the hang of it, and she knew each stove was different, and she'd have had a tough time making a *gut* first impression on her new husband if she'd burned his first meal.

Her heart quickened at the thought of Jacob as her husband, and wondered if she would ever be able to fully look him in the eye. One thing was certain; she would beg his forgiveness and confess everything to him when they spoke later today as he'd promised. Amish did not divorce but in very rare occasions, but she didn't fear that. She feared a lifetime with a man who would not be able to forgive her for forcing him into a marriage that he didn't ask for. But she was determined to spend her lifetime making it up to him, and doing her best to prevent him from regretting his decision to go along with the marriage.

Distracted by her own thoughts of the man she'd yearned for since her youth, she burned the back of her hand on the edge of the stove as she pulled the second batch of muffins from the oven. She immediately dropped the pan on the stove and let out a whine.

Jacob entered in through the kitchen door and spotted Lizzie's clumsiness with the pan and went to her aid when he realized she'd burned her hand.

He drew her hand into his, examining the redness that was already forming a small white blister. He steered her over toward the sink and turned on the cold faucet, pushing her hand under the water. She continued to whine a little, but hadn't looked up at him. When she did, she gasped at the sight of blood dripping down both sides of his chin.

"What on earth happened to you? You're bleeding!"

He shook off her worry. "I cut myself shaving."

Lizzie's heart did a flip-flop in her chest. If he'd shaved, did that mean he hadn't taken their marriage seriously? As a married Amish man, he was to grow out his *baard*. Had he changed his mind overnight, and had intentions to go to the Bishop and have the marriage annulled? Lizzie's heart ached as he held her hand under the stream of water from the kitchen faucet. His nearness made her desire him even more, but she quickly hardened her heart against the fearful thought that she might not be married to him much longer. Pulling her hand away, she ushered him to the table and wrapped her hand in a water-drenched tea-towel.

ಬಂದ

Jacob noticed the sudden stiffness in Lizzie's body-language, and her sudden urgency for him to let go of her hand. Had he pushed her too far by taking her hand into his? He wondered why she suddenly pulled her hand away. Did she think it too forward even for them as a married couple? He'd enjoyed the softness of her skin, but he feared she may not want him to be a husband to her in every way. Was she with the *Englisch* so long that her heart had forgotten the gentleness of Amish love? He feared the meal she'd made for him was only a gesture to appease him and go through the motions of her wifely duties. As he searched her averting gaze, he wondered if she regretted marrying him, and had intent to confess the entire truth to the Bishop, and then ask for an annulment.

Feeling discouraged, he sat down at the head of the table and waited for her to sit beside him. When she did, he bowed his head for the silent prayer.

Dear Gott, denki for this wonderful bounty of food my new fraa has prepared for my familye. I ask you to bless our marriage even though we did not enter into it with pure hearts. I will honor her as I said in my vows, and will love her as you intended. Please do not put doubt in our minds for this marriage, but give us the strength to endure whatever trials you put before us as atonement for our sinful actions.

CHAPTER 14

Abby felt jealousy rise up in her at the sight of Jacob walking into the barn with Caleb hoisted on his shoulder. She stood up from playing with the kittens and walked toward Caleb's horse. She reached up and caressed his soft nose, her back to her dad and brother. Anger finally claimed her as she listened to them converse and joke with each other.

Abby whirled around to meet her dad's eye. "When can I have my own horse? Caleb said you would buy me one."

Jacob tried not to let her tone alert him, but spoke calmly in response. "We can go to the auction on Saturday if you'd like, and you can pick one out then. But you must spend the week learning from Caleb how to care for a horse. If you're ready by Saturday, then we will go in search of a gentle horse that I will teach you how to break."

Abby scrunched up her face. "What do ya mean "break"? Will I have to hurt it? Cuz my mom says we should always be kind to animals."

Jacob chuckled at Abby's naïve approach to farm life, and wondered if a week would be enough time to teach her all there was to know about caring for a horse.

"To break a horse means to train it. And no, it won't hurt the horse. It is not the Amish way to hurt any animal, so your *mamm* was correct in her instruction."

"How long do I have to wait for my new cell phone? My friends are probably worried about me by now since they haven't heard from me for three days."

Jacob feared a conversation with his new *dochder* about the use of phones and television, and other *Englisch* devices. "The Amish don't use phones except in emergency situations. Some members of the community have phones in their barns, but I don't. I thought your *mamm* explained to you about that."

Abby crossed her arms. "When my phone got shut off cuz she wouldn't pay the bill, she said I could get a new phone once we settled in Indiana. Are you telling me you aren't gonna let me have one?"

Jacob tried to choose his words carefully, so as not to alienate Abby. "When you enter your *rumspringa* you may choose to get a phone. But for now, we will have no more talk of it."

"I thought having a father was going to be fun. You could at least *try* to spoil me!" Abby stormed off, tears spilling from her porcelain cheeks.

If this is one my trials, Gott, then I accept it with a willing spirit. But please bless me with the strength to endure the kind's wrath, and bless me with the words to break her like the wild horse that the Englisch ways have implanted themselves in her spirit.

৪৩৪৩

Lizzie set herself to making beds after doing the noon dishes. Jacob had excused himself after the noon meal to go into town, and she hoped he still intended to fulfill his promise to purchase a new bed even though he hadn't mentioned it specifically. Caleb stayed behind to work with Abby in the barn—something about teaching her how to care for the horse. Lizzie was too preoccupied to pay any attention, and wasn't concerned unless they were getting into trouble, which she didn't think they would do since Caleb seemed to be a well-behaved child.

Noting the house could use a good sweeping with the broom, and the rugs looked like they desperately needed to be hung on the clothesline so she could smack the dirt off of them, Lizzie made use of the time that Jacob was gone to surprise him with a clean home when he returned. A small part of her felt a little strange cleaning another woman's home, but it was her home now and she would take pride in keeping it clean. It was the way of the Amish that she automatically took over the duties as the new *fraa,* but it didn't keep the little butterflies from fluttering in her stomach for fear that she may move something that was sacred memorabilia of Nellie's.

She and Nellie had been friends before she left the community, so why did she feel jealousy over the woman even though she was deceased? Perhaps because the woman had been the first to love Jacob, while she'd lost her virtue after Eddie had spiked her drink, and had no recollection of the act. The thought of it made her shutter. And even though she'd never had relations again with any man, she hoped Jacob wouldn't view her as damaged goods.

Her *daed* assumed Jacob had been the one to compromise her virtue and that was how Abby had come into the world—she'd been violated, but it was a hazy memory at best. She couldn't help but wonder what Jacob must think about her to accuse him of being the one doing the violating—but that sort of thing was not in his nature, even if she'd been the type of girl to provoke such an action from him. He was a good man, and she felt fortunate that he'd taken the blame for her mistake.

If only she knew the real reason why…

&OCK

Jacob was happy that he'd been able to convince the manager of the mattress store to deliver the new bed this afternoon. He wasn't happy it had cost him an extra fifty dollars to convince the man, but he didn't think he could endure sleeping on the floor another night. And he wasn't about to begin his marriage on a sour note by sleeping in the bed he'd shared with Nellie in order to preserve his own sleep and aching back. It was better this way. So why did he feel so funny about his purchase?

His heart quickened at the thought of sleeping so near Lizzie, and wondered if she would expect him to fulfill his husbandly duties to her right away. Normally, time spent directly after a wedding in the community was spent visiting *familye*, but given the abruptness of their wedding, and the fact they had two *kinner* to think about, visiting was not going to be a part of their initial acquaintance with one another as a couple. He was grateful for that much, as he wasn't looking forward to the dinner with Lizzie's *familye* on Saturday. He was also happy this upcoming Sunday was an off-Sunday for the community, and he would not have to face the Bishop or the Elders of the church for another ten days when the next church service would take place.

At least the time at home with his new *familye* would afford him a chance to try to make amends with Lizzie and Abby, who seemed to have a rebellious streak most likely from spending so much time with the *Englisch*. He wondered how the *kind* would be during a Sunday service, and if it would be a struggle to get Abby to accept the faith of the community. He prayed that things would go smoothly and the natural course of getting to know each other would fall into place as though they'd always been a *familye*. Though he knew his reasons for the marriage were to preserve both of their honors in the community, he still couldn't help but feel anxious over his hasty decision to marry Lizzie, and wondered if it would last.

CHAPTER 15

By the time Jacob returned home that evening, it was dusk, and Lizzie had been keeping the evening meal warm and the *kinner* occupied—especially Abby, who didn't understand why they had to wait for Jacob so she could eat. Abby wasn't used to being on a schedule or having to wait for family to sit and have a meal together. In a lot of ways, Lizzie regretted not being a little more strict with her *dochder*. It would have made the transition into the Amish community and lifestyle more pleasant. She knew it was her own fault the *kind* was whining, and hoped it wasn't too late to train her to the strict ways she would now have to live by.

Lizzie looked out the kitchen window at her husband as he greeted a delivery truck in the driveway. Two young men exited the plain white truck and began to unload a mattress and box-spring from the back. Lizzie's heart skipped a beat. Jacob had done as he'd promised, and they could begin their marriage with a bed of their own. She was delighted when the delivery men took away the old bed, but she hoped Jacob, who'd remained expressionless when they removed them, was not experiencing it as a loss. His lack of beard had been an outward sign that his mourning period had ended even though very few widowed Amish men shaved, but she still felt unsure of his feelings, and knew that only time would tell how he was dealing with it.

When all the excitement had passed, and the delivery men had left, Lizzie pulled the evening meal back out of the oven where it had been warming for nearly an hour and set it on the table. It was getting late, and though she was very tired, she was suddenly very wary of bedtime.

ဆဝ၄ဒ

Lizzie made the new bed with the linens and quilt that her *aenti* had given her for her wedding dowry. And since the bedding store had thrown in two new pillows with the purchase, they would have a fresh new start to their life together. Most traces of Nellie had been removed from the house many years ago as far as Lizzie could see, or maybe it was possible that since they had only been married for ten months before she passed that she hadn't had enough time to make her mark on the home in the way that years of marriage would have done. Either way,

Lizzie intended to make her mark on the home starting with the linens; she intended to make the bedroom a place they could eventually connect—at least she hoped so.

Jacob walked in the room and grabbed the other side of the sheet and tucked it into the corner. "I put the *kinner* to bed, but your *dochder* asked if you would tuck her in."

Lizzie looked at him as he grabbed the other side of the quilt and helped, then fitted a pillow case to the other pillow and set it on the bed. It was the first time she'd really looked him over since they'd married the day before. His eyes were kind, but held a hint of apprehension in their reflection. He smiled, and then pushed down his suspenders and pulled his blue dress shirt over his head exposing his muscular flesh. His abs were so defined, Lizzie wondered if he spent his days working out at a gym. She felt heat rising up her neck until it reached her cheeks. Her gaze fell a little wondering if he intended to undress fully in front of her. The smirk on his face showed that he did if she didn't vacate the room or turn around.

She cleared her throat. "I think I'll go tuck Abby in and read her a story. I'll be back in a few minutes."

She quickly exited the room before she was tempted to stare at Jacob any longer. She knew he was her husband, and she was allowed to see him without his clothing, but she wasn't sure she was ready for that yet. Her one-time, short-lived experience with the opposite sex had not prepared her for what would certainly be an inevitable part of their marriage. Jacob had been married long enough to gain some experience, and she worried she would be clumsy and inadequately prepared. There was also the possibility of becoming pregnant again since her first and only experience had brought Abby into her life. Was she prepared for another child? Did she even want anymore? Did Jacob? Amish didn't use birth-control, so she would have to discuss the possibility of children with him—perhaps before they decided to consummate the marriage.

Perhaps some prayer would be in order as well.

ಙೇಬ

Jacob couldn't help but smile when Lizzie exited the room so hastily. He knew it wasn't right to infuriate his new bride, but he reveled in the blush that had claimed her cheeks. He didn't intend to torture her with teasing, but he didn't mind making her squirm a little for forcing him into marrying her. But he had to admit, he could have done worse if he'd picked his own *fraa.* He'd already noticed she didn't appear to have cut her hair the way most Amish girls do when they go out to live among the *Englisch,* and Abby had the same long, light brown hair and blue eyes as her *mudder.* It would be tough to keep to himself physically since he was very attracted to Lizzie, but he needed to be sure she was committed to the marriage for the right reasons before he would consider consummating.

&

Lizzie took her time with Abby, talking to her about school. She wasn't happy about the school being so small, but she was happy to hear she wouldn't be expected to go until the harvest was brought in which would amount to at least another month. Until then, Caleb would work with *their* father, and Abby would work alongside her at the B&B making beds and doing dishes. Abby groaned at the thought of doing chores, but she also knew it would be another opportunity to sample more of the cookies, pies and pastries Aunt Bess kept on hand for her guests. Abby was intrigued with the baked goods, and wanted to learn to make them herself.

When Lizzie returned to the room she now shared with Jacob, she was happy that the lamps had been turned down, and he seemed to be sleeping. She sank to the corner of the room and dressed in her nightie as discretely as she could, and then slipped carefully under the quilt.

Jacob turned to her. "I purchased some fabric when I was in town so you could sew some dresses and night clothes for you and Abby. I also got you a treadle sewing machine and placed it in the front room just before I came up here for the evening."

Well there it was—open confirmation of his disapproval. Lizzie's heart slammed against her ribcage.

"*Denki,*" she said quietly before rolling over and closing her eyes against the tears that were pushing a lump into her throat.

It probably would have been more obvious if he'd just come right out and said he's ashamed of the way I dress! But at least he got me a sewing machine!

CHAPTER 16

Lizzie woke with a stiff neck from sleeping rigidly to avoid accidentally bumping Jacob during the night. When she turned over in the bed, he was already gone and the sheet was cold, indicating he'd been up for some time. She lay there for a minute, wondering if there would ever be a time when he would linger under the quilt and hold her before getting up for the day. She pushed the silly, romantic notion aside, feeling defeated by their present living situation. They were going through the motions of marriage, but had no closeness or intimacy as would be the norm for a newly married couple.

She forced herself out from under the warm quilt and set her foot on the chilly wood floor. The rain she'd heard several hours ago had no-doubt cooled the temperature, but she hoped it would warm soon. Her *daed* had promised that he would give her the contents of her things they'd stored away in the barn after she'd left, and she hoped her cloak and aprons would still fit her. She didn't expect her dresses to still fit since she'd been a scrawny teenager, and her figure had grown womanly curves at her hips and bust when she had Abby.

As she dressed for the day in the work dress her *aenti* had given her, she made mental note of the chores she would have to complete before leaving for the B&B at one o'clock. Check-out time was at noon, and Aunt Bess served a noon meal before the guests left, so Lizzie could begin cleaning the rooms, and then wash the noon dishes. She was happy that Jacob hadn't objected to her obligation to her *aenti,* but she was happier she'd have money to contribute for the household expenses, especially since Jacob had married her and was now responsible for her as her provider. Knowing that she could help eased some of the guilt over pushing him into the responsibility.

Another silent breakfast ensued between Lizzie and Jacob, while the children filled the air with chatter over the ducks in the pond and the changing leaves on the trees. Lizzie was grateful for the innocent conversation of the *kinner,* because it allowed her to study her husband's reaction to her *dochder.* His responses to their questions were gentle and attentive, and he smiled often. Lizzie's heart beat rapidly in her chest thinking about what a kind and loving man he was. It was those very same traits that made her fall in love with him when they were young.

ༀ

Jacob didn't like the silence between him and Lizzie, but he was grateful for the *kinner* to fill the gap between them. He'd caught her watching him several times throughout the morning meal, but didn't know how to incorporate her in the conversation. They'd conversed through the *kinner,* and he admired the gentleness in her tone when she spoke to them. Her smile was genuine when she addressed their constant questions, and he liked the way her dimples lit up her face. He'd fallen in love with that dimpled smile when they were young, so why was he having so much trouble connecting her to that girl now? Was his heart still so reserved from the heartache of her leaving him then? He tried reasoning with himself that the thought was unsubstantiated, but maybe he needed to address the subject of forgiveness a little more closely during his prayer time.

ༀ

The sun rested high above their heads as Lizzie and Abby walked the mile from their new home to the B&B. The last of the season's blackbirds flitted in the colorful trees overhead, which provided a canopy of shade for part of the journey. Jacob and Caleb had long-since traveled to neighboring farms to help bring in the harvest. Being at the Hockstetler farm, Jacob had boasted about the large pumpkin crop, and promised to bring a few home with him for pies.

Lizzie hoped there would be enough for her to can some so they would have use of the pumpkin for Christmas pies in addition to the apples she planned on canning from the two apple trees she'd noticed on the other side of the barn. She hoped her skills as a homemaker would prove to Jacob she was capable of being a good Amish *fraa.*

Abby picked up a rock in the dirt road and tossed it ahead of them for the third time. "Do I have to start calling you *mamm* like Caleb does?"

The question caught Lizzie off guard, but she was glad Abby brought up the subject. "I would like it if you could learn the language of the Amish people. I feel bad that I never taught you before now. It was wrong of me to keep your heritage from you; I should have been teaching you from the beginning."

"Why did you run away from my father? Did you hate him?"

Lizzie's heart nearly fell to her shoes. "No, Abby. I loved him very much, but I didn't think he loved me back. I acted in haste and didn't think things through. I'm grateful for the time I spent away from the Amish community because it taught me a valuable lesson."

Abby picked up the rock again when they came upon it in the road. After tossing it again, she looked up at Lizzie and squinted her eyes against the sun. "Am I supposed to be learning a lesson by giving up my life in Ohio to stay here?"

Lizzie swallowed hard, choosing her words carefully. "Remember a few days ago how afraid you were to get on the bus to come here? I told you that you would learn to love it here. I'm hoping that's what you'll learn by being here. The Amish are a gentle people—not at all like the troublesome people we've encountered in the past few months."

"You mean that Eddie guy? Who was he anyway, and why did I hear him say he was going to take me away from you?"

Lizzie felt her knees buckle at the question, and she slowed her pace to keep her balance. "He was a bad man that thought he could force me to give him money to pay for his mistakes. I met him just after I left home. I was a stupid kid back then, and I didn't make good decisions about who I made friends with. I'm glad that part of my life is over, and I'm glad to be back with people who really love me."

"Like Jacob—my dad?"

Lizzie smiled nervously at Abby's question, but she was too young to understand the circumstances of her mother's marriage. Lizzie hoped in time Jacob would forgive her and learn to love her, but she knew that despite her relationship with him, he would be a *gut vadder* to Abby, and that was all that mattered to her at the moment.

CHAPTER 17

Though Lizzie missed her work as a pharmacy technician, she discovered that she enjoyed working alongside Abby at the B&B even more. Lizzie was proud of her for being so much help with very little complaining. Her day would have dragged by if her *dochder* would have rebelled against the work that needed to be done. She discovered after the first guest room that Abby preferred to do the dusting and sweeping with the broom over the making of the beds. In her defense, she did not have long enough arms to spread the linens across the mattresses.

Lizzie giggled at her first attempt, and wondered if it was too late in life to begin training Abby in the Amish ways in order to make them stay with her into her adulthood. Visions of her *rumspringa* made Lizzie shudder at the thought of her little Abby running off the way she had. It made her think of her *daed,* and she wondered if he would ever feel he could trust her again.

After three steady hours of work making certain each room was prepared for new guests that would arrive shortly, and for those that had stayed on at the B&B, Lizzie took pride in the ache that had crept into the small of her back, knowing she'd earned it for the hard work that made her feel at home.

When they returned to the farm, Abby ran down to the pond where Caleb was chasing the ducks. It made Lizzie giggle to watch him running after them, their feathers flying and squawking so loudly she wondered if they were enjoying the game or in fear for their lives. With the children occupied, she thought she might take a few minutes before she needed to prepare the evening meal to try to talk to her new husband. As she entered the double doors that hung open, she heard whistling from the other side of the horse stalls and followed the sound of the familiar hymn.

Lizzie stopped in her tracks when she spotted Jacob leaning over a wash stand on a table. His back turned away from her, she stood and watched him shave, admiring the muscles that chiseled out his bare back. She crept a little closer, hoping she wouldn't startle him for fear he would cut his chin the way he had the day before. Curious as to why he continued to shave, she felt irritation rise up in her. As a married man, he should not be shaving. But would she complain, knowing she liked his clean-shaven look? But what would the community think if he should continue to shave instead of growing a beard? Would they question the legitimacy of their marriage?

Before she could reason with her questions, Jacob turned to face her. "You don't have to sneak up on me. If you want to watch me shave, you're more than welcome to."

Lizzie's face turned a deep shade of red. Was he trying to provoke her? "I wasn't trying to sneak up on you; I just didn't want to startle you. I didn't want you cutting your throat open."

He set the towel down and turned around, his suspenders dangling at his sides, and his well-muscled chest and abdomen enticed her. She wondered if he was intentionally teasing her, and the smirk on his face indicated he probably was. She could feel the heat rising up to her cheeks, and her voice was shaky when she tried to speak. "I was hoping we could spend a minute talking before I went in and cooked the evening meal. I didn't mean to interrupt you."

His smile deepened, exposing the tiny lines that had formed on his manly face. She studied him for a moment, realizing how handsome he'd become in the past ten years. He took a step toward her, his eyes fixed on hers, and stood close enough that she could smell the flecks of shaving soap that clung to his face. She wanted to reach out and touch him, but she didn't want to break the spell that lingered between them.

"*Mamm,* Abby needs you!"

Caleb's sudden burst startled Lizzie, and the way he addressed her almost seemed foreign.

She turned her head from Jacob, breaking the spell.

"Is she hurt?"

"She got too close to the duck nest in the reeds and her foot is stuck."

All three of them ran to the edge of the pond, where Abby whined, her arm outstretched toward the duck nest.

She looked up into Jacob's face, who was wading in the water to get to her. "I can't reach the babies, Dad, and I want one."

Jacob reached down and untangled her foot, scooping her up in his arms. "Those babies have to stay with their *mudder,* just like you have to stay with yours. You could have drowned, Abby. Promise me you won't go out that far among the reeds ever again."

She leaned his head against his shoulder and he hugged her tight until he reached the grassy edge of the pond. "I won't. I promise."

Lizzie felt a tear glide down her cheek. She was happy that the two had bonded over such a simple thing, and Abby hadn't talked back. But most endearing was the gentleness with which Jacob had spoken to her daughter. He was truly a loving man, and she couldn't have asked God Himself for a better man to be her husband and the father of her child.

80G3

After Abby was all dried, she ran downstairs to help Lizzie prepare the evening meal. She rolled out dough for biscuits, and used an upside down glass to cut the circles of dough.

"How come you never asked me to help you cook before? I like cooking."

Surprised to hear such a statement from Abby, she smiled happily. "I guess we just never had the time to make big meals."

"But we did more work today than I've ever seen you do, and we still had time to cook breakfast and now dinner."

Lizzie picked up the baking pan full of freshly cut biscuits and placed them in the oven. "Things are different here. You work hard, but everything you do is for your family—to feed them and care for their needs."

"I'm not happy about not being able to watch TV, but there's so much more to do here, I didn't even miss it today."

Lizzie smiled knowingly, wondering why she'd ever left the community.

CHAPTER 18

Lizzie could barely keep her eyes open as she finished the last stitch on her new nightgown. Everyone had been asleep for at least two hours, but she'd wanted to finish it before retiring. She didn't want to cause anymore discomfort to her husband by wearing the summery nightie anymore for fear that it appeared too worldly for an appropriate Amish *fraa* to wear. Not to mention the scowl on his face when he went for his robe and saw that she was still wearing it. She supposed he was set in his ways, and having her invade his space would take some getting used to, but that didn't stop her from thinking it a little funny that he was so territorial.

Creeping up the stairs as quietly as she could, she forgot which one of the stairs squeaked until it was too late. She remained still for a moment, listening to be sure she hadn't disturbed anyone in the house. When all remained quiet, she proceeded to her room and slipped beneath the quilt.

Jacob rolled over toward her, and before she could put her back to him, his arm slipped across her stomach, his head resting on her shoulder. Panic pushed her heart rate to its limits, and she wondered if she could roll away from him without waking him. If he woke up, it would be awkward, and might give him ammunition to tease her later. He nestled his head a little, leaving her wondering if he was connecting with her on a subconscious level, or if he was merely used to roaming around an empty bed and had no idea he was cuddling her. Either way, she didn't dare move for fear of disturbing him. She closed her eyes, and tried to calm her heart rate, but she couldn't breathe. She took a few deep breaths, feeling like she wasn't getting enough air; she had to roll over on her side before she hyperventilated so much she passed out.

With one smooth roll, she was on her side with her back to him. No sooner had she settled in position and caught her breath, than Jacob moved closer to her, pulling her into a spooning position with the strong arm that still circled her waist. His warm breath on the back of her neck tickled her spine, and she had to admit she didn't mind the closeness of her husband. She'd spent many a lonely night lying awake over her adult years wishing for a moment like this with a husband, and now she was experiencing it. It was nice, even if Jacob wasn't aware of what he was doing.

In the morning, Jacob was missing from the bed as he had the previous mornings. She had no idea what time he got up every day, but it was obviously what he was used to doing. She wondered if he'd woken while he was still cuddling her, or if he was completely unaware of the contact that had taken place overnight. Her heart fluttered at the thought of it. Dressing quickly, she ran down the stairs to prepare a big morning meal, knowing the cold weather would drive up her husband's appetite. She'd felt a closeness with him last night, and she would do whatever it took to make the marriage right, even if all she could do was cook and clean for him for the time being, but she would do it as any good Amish *fraa* would.

When everyone was seated at the table for breakfast, Jacob bowed his head for the silent prayer. Abby bowed her head, and Lizzie was delighted that she seemed eager to participate in some of the simple traditions already.

Jacob went for his second helping of pancakes and looked over at Lizzie with a smile. "We will be going to the Beiler's today for the barn-raising. I'd like it if you and Abby would join me and Caleb. Your help will be needed with the preparation of meals and cleanup."

Lizzie's heart skipped a beat at the invitation, and she accepted with a nod. It was normal for the wives to accompany their husbands during working bees, and this would be their first as a married couple. She hoped it meant he was beginning to accept her as his wife, and that he intended to portray that to the community. But the fact remained that he was still shaving his beard and they'd been married for four days already.

Jacob turned to Abby. "Do you think you're ready to go to auction tomorrow and pick out a pony?"

Abby nearly jumped out of her seat. "Do you mean it, Dad?"

He smiled at Lizzie, and then looked back at Abby whose eyes were wide as saucers. "Caleb says you've been a good student to his instruction on how to care for the horses. I think we can get you your own horse so you can learn to ride too."

Abby leaped from her chair and swung her arms around Jacob's neck. "Thank you, Dad. I promise I'll take real good care of it. You won't have to yell at me or anything!"

Jacob sent a confused look to Lizzie at Abby's statement. She hoped he didn't think she had yelled at Abby in the past. Her punishment of the child had consisted of a time-out chair, and she herself wondered if Abby had perhaps been scolded inappropriately at the public school. Shrugging it off for now, she lifted herself from her chair and asked Abby to help with the dishes. If they were to get an early start to the barn-raising, Lizzie would need to hurry with the necessary chores and put together some food to take along to share with the community.

৪৩৫৪

Lizzie's stomach filled with butterflies as the gentle rocking of the buggy bumped her into Jacob repeatedly. Abby and Caleb sat in the back chattering non-stop about the puppies at the Beiler farm with which Caleb was certain Jacob would permit him to bring one of them home with them at the end of the day. Lizzie was too preoccupied with thoughts of Jacob being so near, and nervousness over her first community appearance as Jacob's *fraa*. She knew the women would accept her, and she probably knew a lot of them already from school, but it was going to be awkward as they tested her for signs that she had become too *Englisch* while she had been away from the community.

CHAPTER 19

From the look of the crowd that had already gathered at the Beiler farm, they were late, even though it was only seven o'clock. The sun had not been up for long, but the neighbors seemed eager to get the barn-raising underway. Jonah and Rebecca Beiler greeted them with their *mamm,* Martha, when they pulled into the yard that was already crowded with buggies and plenty of children running around.

Before taking his horse to the large area of shade trees with the other horses, Jacob made a few introductions. "This is my *fraa,* Elizabeth, and my *dochder,* Abby."

Lizzie held a hand out to Martha, trying to place her. She was slightly in shock at hearing Jacob refer to Abby as his daughter. It was something that would take some getting used to, but she supposed now was as good a time as any to establish their place.

"*Wie gehts,* Elizabeth?"

"Please, call me Lizzie."

Martha nodded acceptance of the nickname, and directed them toward a group of women from the community already preparing a feast big enough to feed two communities. "*Kume,* join us while we prepare meals for our *familye.*"

Abby clung to Lizzie's side despite the promptings from Caleb, Rebecca and Jonah to play a quick game of tag before they would be expected to cart tools and supplies to their *daeds* during the building process. Lizzie preferred to have Abby at her side; if nothing else, she was a shield for the prying questions she was sure to endure throughout the day from the other women. She noticed her own *daed* and *bruder* were not in attendance, but she'd heard from Aunt Bess that his own farm was a struggle for him since he'd aged in recent years. Seth would be needed to help at home with their *daed* until he would take a wife, but Lizzie had the feeling he would stay on even after he was married. It was the Amish way, and she chided herself for not staying to keep house for him in her *mamm's* absence.

As the day wore on, Lizzie relaxed more with the women, and even accepted an invitation to a quilting bee the following week to begin the wedding dowries for the young girls in the community who would be marrying in the upcoming wedding season, which was nearly upon them.

ಬಂಡ

Abby and Caleb were asleep by the time they reached home that night. Caleb woke up enough to walk into the house, but Abby was so worn out, Jacob picked her up and took her up to her room. Lizzie followed, watching as her husband placed a gentle kiss on Abby's forehead after tucking her under the quilts.

Jacob moved past her as he exited Abby's room. "I have to unhitch the horse. I'll be in when I've given him a good rubdown."

Lizzie hunched her shoulders thinking she could use a good rubdown herself. She was tired and ached all over. She could only imagine how much more Jacob must be sore from the hard day he'd put in. They'd managed to get the frame and the roof finished. The interior work would be up to Adam Beiler and his son, Jonah, who was a year older than Abby.

Lizzie readied herself for bed, and then went downstairs to make a fresh pot of coffee for Jacob. A chill had blown in from the north earlier in the afternoon, and the ride home in the dark had chilled her to the bone; she could only imagine how cold Jacob was up on the roof for so many hours, unprotected from the strong gusts of wind.

Just as she had finished pouring herself a cup, the door flew open with a cold rush of air. Jacob entered shivering, and she handed him the cup she'd meant for herself. He sat at the table and wrapped both hands around the steaming cup, and sipped it. Lizzie poured another cup and sat beside him.

"*Denki* for the *kaffi*. It's gotten pretty cold in the last couple of hours. I was hoping the weather would hold out until we could finish the harvest."

Lizzie looked up into his blue-green eyes, afraid to say what was on her mind, but they hadn't talked about anything personal yet, and she was beginning to worry they would always have a very formal marriage that centered around the children, and community obligations. Did he really see her as his wife and Abby as his daughter, or was he doing what was expected of him in order to maintain his position in the community?

Jacob cleared his throat. "I'd like to take you for a buggy ride tomorrow evening after we return from the auction."

Lizzie's heart rate sped up at the thought of it. She wasn't going to argue if he was reaching out to her, but buggy rides were for courting and they were not courting—they were married. It suddenly dawned on her why he was shaving—he intended to court her. Excitement rose in the depths of her belly over his offer.

"That would be lovely. I'd like that."

Lovely? Did she just say the word *lovely* to Jacob?

He nodded and rose from his chair and rinsed his coffee cup at the sink, and then left the room. She heard the squeak of the steps, and decided it was best if she stayed downstairs and took care of the pot of coffee before going up—she would give him time to fall asleep before retiring for the evening.

CHAPTER 20

Lizzie woke up with Jacob's arm laying across her waist, his ankle crossing hers, and his head wedged in the crook of her neck. She chided herself for drinking that second cup of coffee because she had to use the bathroom, and Jacob had her trapped beneath him. If she moved, she would surely wake him, but she was close to wetting the bed if she didn't break free from him. She tried rolling over on her side the way she had the night before, but he pulled her closer just like he had before. The only thing she could do was to risk disturbing him before her bladder burst.

With one quick movement, she slid to the edge of the bed and stood up. Looking back, he seemed undisturbed, and Lizzie let out a sigh of relief before tip-toeing out of the room. When she returned, she tried slipping back under the quilt without shivering, but the house was a little chilly.

"Is everything alright?" Jacob whispered in a raspy voice.

Her back was to him, but she was worried that he'd be upset with her for waking him. "I'm fine. I'm sorry for disturbing you."

"You shouldn't drink *kaffi* so close to bedtime. You're shivering. *Kume,* let me warm you up." He pulled her close, wrapping his strong arms around her.

Lizzie couldn't help but smile at his invitation. She scooted back toward him and allowed him to cradle her in the warmth of his body. Nothing more was said between them, but Lizzie suddenly felt protected and safe for the first time in years.

ഇന്ദ്രം

At the auction, Jacob hoisted Caleb and Abby on each of his broad shoulders so they could get a better look at the horses they considered bidding on. Jacob had allowed Abby to choose three, and they now waited for the best price. Satisfied with the price he'd bid on the solid white gelding, Jacob waited for a counter-bid, but there was none. Abby ran happily to claim her prize while Jacob paid the auctioneer, and Lizzie delighted in watching the father-daughter interaction between Jacob and Abby.

After he willingly cuddled her last night, she was looking at him a little differently—almost with love. She had to admit that being in his arms had stirred some unresolved feelings of the past, and she wondered if he felt it too as he looked back at her with a wide grin spread across his lips. She could get lost in that smile if she wasn't careful. Before she knew his intentions for their marriage, she would keep a lock on her heart. She felt suddenly very fragile and exposed, not wanting to be hurt again where Jacob was concerned.

ଔଔ

Jacob felt like a teenager again as he smiled at Lizzie. It was almost as if no time had passed, and they were young again, and ready to explore where their future could take them. But as Caleb and Abby crowded around his sides, the new horse tagging along, reality set in, and he realized his obligation to his *familye* needed a stronger base than a teenage crush. He may not have asked for this *familye,* but it was his responsibility now, and he would find a way to keep his feelings in check until he could establish where Lizzie's loyalties stood before giving his heart so freely again. He hadn't stopped loving her. That was obvious to him when he took her in his arms the night before. But unless she intended to return those feelings, he would remain reserved for the sake of his obligation.

ଔଔ

Abby whined all the way home, complaining the jostling of the buggy was making her feel sick. When they finally pulled into the yard, Jacob instructed Caleb to tie up the buggy and lead the new horse into the barn so he could take Abby to her bed. No sooner had he picked her up out of the buggy when she let loose the contents of her stomach down his shirt. Lizzie rushed to his aid apologetically, but he whisked Abby into the house. Lizzie grabbed towels from the mud room off the kitchen and wet them in the sink, hoping she could catch most of the mess before it made a trail to Abby's room.

Jacob placed Abby gently in her bed and removed her shoes. Smoothing back her hair, he whispered something Lizzie couldn't make out, but it caused the corners of her daughter's lips to turn up slightly. It was tough for Lizzie to allow Jacob to take control over her daughter, but it was a nice change from the burden she'd shouldered alone for the past ten years.

Jacob squeezed Abby's hand. "You get some rest after your *mamm* puts some dry clothes on you. Caleb and I will tend to your horse and you can visit with him in the morning before service."

She nodded; her smile fading as he left the room.

CHAPTER 21

Even though Lizzie was a little sad she and Jacob had missed out on their chance to take a buggy ride, she was too tired by the time she settled Abby down and got her back to sleep. Though she was certain Abby suffered only from a case of motion-sickness, she wouldn't take the chance that it was more and leave her just to spend some time courting her husband. The thought of it made her giggle. She was certain it was the first time that a husband and wife would spend the beginning of their marriage courting one another, but she hoped they would get another chance soon.

With the stress of a full day ahead of them, Lizzie turned in before Jacob came in from tending to the horses. She was nearly asleep when she felt him slip under the quilt and move in close to her.

"I'm sorry I was too tired to make you *kaffi*." Lizzie mumbled.

He nuzzled her neck and kissed her lightly. "I think we had a full day, and we could both use some rest."

He kissed her again, sending shivers down her spine. She wanted to turn and kiss him full on the mouth, but she feared rejection if he considered her too forward from living among the *Englisch* too long. As tough as it was, she would wait for him to make the advances. Even as slow as they came, she was satisfied for now knowing he desired to have some closeness with her. On the other hand, what if he wanted to consummate their marriage, and she kept her back to him sending him the signal she was uninterested? She turned slightly to see if he would make another advance, but to her dismay, he was already asleep.

༂ౚᏟ౩

Jacob had a tough time keeping his mind on the church service that morning. He couldn't believe he'd been bold enough to kiss the back of Lizzie's neck twice last night, but he knew his defenses were down because of being over-tired. He knew she was tired too, but she hadn't pushed him away. In fact, she had moved closer to him each night. Maybe it was time for him to come clean about the real reason he'd married her. As much as he'd tried to reason with himself at the time, it wasn't because Caleb needed a new *mamm,* or to spare his reputation in the community; it was because he'd never gotten over her. She was his first love, and he couldn't help but feel that the circle of life had brought them back together. He no longer carried the guilt over Nellie's passing; he knew it wasn't his fault, and there was nothing he could have done to prevent it from happening. It was *Gotte's wille.*

Before he realized, they had gotten through their first service as a *familye,* and every time he looked back at Abby, she seemed to be content. Lizzie had even smiled at him from the other side of the room where she sat with his new *dochder.* He'd whispered a silent prayer of thanks for Abby, knowing that if not for her, he wouldn't be married to Lizzie. Thinking about it though, he knew he needed to find out from her once and for all why she'd placed his name on Abby's *Englisch* birth certificate. He guessed there were several things they needed to work out before they could move forward into a relationship. There could be no secrets between them—even the one he'd harbored for the past ten years.

⁎⁎⁎

"Your dad is my grandpa, right?" Abby was asking from the back of the buggy on the way to her father's farm.

"Yes, Abby." Lizzie's voice cracked at the admission. In all the time she'd been away, she never once gave thought to what her own father was missing out on by not knowing about Abby. She was, after all, his first grandchild, and she'd denied them both the opportunity to be a family. Guilt made her heart flutter, and she wondered if the strictness in her father's tone would carry over to the dinner they were about to encounter at his house. She hadn't intended to disappoint her father, or stain her mother's memory, but that's how it looked in the eyes of her father, and she hoped marrying Jacob and joining the church would eventually make things right between them. She knew that a good start would be to teach Abby all she could about the Amish, and to make sure she even learned the language.

Lizzie stiffened her shoulders as they entered her father's house, determined that no matter what he said to her, or no matter how disapproving his tone, she would be respectful and show Abby a good example of how to properly yield to the authority of a parent.

Her older *bruder,* David, and his *fraa,* Leah, had not yet arrived with her nephew. To her surprise, her *daed* and younger *bruder,* Seth, greeted her with open arms and smiles. Was it because she was married? Or did they do it out of respect for Jacob only? At the moment, she didn't care; she was home, and this was the happiest she'd been in a long time.

ೋღ

Abby already saw the advantages to having a grandpa—*Grossdaddi*—as he'd taught her to say.

Seeing the never-ending smile spread across her mom's—*mamm's*—lips was enough to make any child's heart sing. She watched her *mamm* most of the afternoon, and realized she'd never seen her so happy—*froh*. Her new *Onkel* Seth, and her new *bruder,* Caleb, had spent a good part of the afternoon teaching her a few simple words that would make things easier to understand when eavesdropping on adult conversation—something Seth and Caleb both admitted to enjoying. She was just happy because her *mamm* was happy, and she discovered that having a big *familye* to care about you was more important than having a cell phone or TV—especially now that she had a new *daed*.

CHAPTER 22

Lizzie felt the awkwardness drift away between her and her *daed* the moment he handed her the quilt that her *mamm* had made for her tenth birthday. She'd never gotten the chance to give it to her since she passed away two months before. It was something Lizzie had never known about—until now.

Tears welled up in her eyes at the beautiful, intricate stitching her *mamm* was known for. Her quilts had been the best in the community, and all the women were in awe of her detailed quilts and her eye for matching and arranging the colors and patterns.

"Why didn't you give this to me sooner, *Daed?*"

Hiram cleared his throat. "It was in the attic in a trunk that I just couldn't bring myself to going through until a few years ago. I knew she'd made it for you, but I couldn't look at her things after she died, so I packed them all in the trunk and put them in the attic. He handed her a brown paper bag that was folded at the top.

"I found this in the trunk too. I'd forgotten about it until I went in search of things you might want now that you're married. It's the quilt she started making for the *boppli* before she...well, I thought you might want to finish it and use it when you and Jacob expand your *familye* and have your next *boppli.*"

Her heart skipped a beat at the thought of carrying Jacob's child.

Hiram urged her to take the bag, despite her hesitation.

Lizzie opened the bag, a lump forming in her throat as she pulled out the yellow baby quilt that was nearly finished. Her hands shook as she turned it over, examining each stitch. She held it to her cheek, believing she could almost smell her *mamm* in the folds of the fabric.

"*Denki.* I only hope I can make my stitches as evenly as *mamm's.* She was the best quilter in this community—that's a lot to live up to."

Hiram put his arm across her shoulder. "I have faith in you."

Those few simple words and the affection from her *daed* was all she needed to tell her she was forgiven.

෧෬

The entire ride home, Lizzie's thoughts were occupied with visions of what a new *boppli* would mean to her *daed*. It was clear to her from their conversation that he'd felt cheated out of the joy of helping to raise Abby. He seemed proud to be a *grossdaddi,* and Lizzie did not want to disappoint him further by letting on that she and Jacob had not yet had the opportunity to even create a *boppli*.

Jacob startled her by placing his hand on top of hers. "You seem preoccupied. Did you have an unpleasant conversation with your *daed?"*

"*Nee.* In fact, it was a very good talk. He gave me the quilt my *mamm* was making for the *boppli* she was having before she…"

Jacob squeezed her hand. "That's something very special. I noticed the large quilt on the top of the boxes your *daed* helped me put in the back of the buggy. Is that the one? It's very nice."

Lizzie couldn't help leaning her head on his shoulder for comfort. He put his arm around her to steady her shaking.

"She made that one for my tenth birthday, but she never got the chance to give it to me. She was gone a few months before. The trunk he gave me contains a lot of her things she used in the kitchen, and even some of her personal things. He thought I could use them now that I'm married."

Jacob tightened his grip across her shoulders, holding the reins with his left hand. "You can make it your home by putting your *mamm's* things anywhere you want. I want you and Abby to feel at home there, and I want you to do whatever you need to in order to be comfortable."

Lizzie cuddled in closer to him. "*Denki*. That means a lot to me."

Jacob smiled at her. "I have an idea."

He pulled the buggy into the drive of the B&B instead of continuing on to their farm. "Do you think your *aenti* would agree to stay with the *kinner* for an hour so we can take that buggy ride we missed out on?"

He assisted her down. "I don't see why not. She hasn't seen Abby in a couple of days, and she was going to teach her how to make a snitz pie."

It didn't matter to Lizzie that she was already exhausted from the long day at church, and then the dinner with her *familye,* what mattered was that she was finally going to get the chance to have a *gut* talk with her husband.

CHAPTER 23

Jacob steered the buggy down the ribbon of road, keeping his eye on the large harvest moon that illuminated their path with a romantic, amber glow. Lizzie leaned against him, making it tough for him to break the silence with their long-overdue talk about the circumstances that brought them together as a married couple.

"I'm only curious about one thing. Why did you name me as Abby's *vadder?*"

Lizzie straightened, and Jacob wished he hadn't been so blunt. He enjoyed having her so close to him, but now it was evident that her defenses were up, and he feared they would remain distant until the matter was resolved.

"I was very emotional at the time of her birth because of the circumstances that brought her into existence in the first place. I was alone and scared, and without a midwife, I gave birth in a hospital. They required the legal document, and I was afraid that with such a document as public record of her birth that Eddie, her real father, would take her from me if he knew the truth."

Jacob slowed the horse, looking for a spot to pull over on the side of the dirt road. He didn't want to continue on endlessly because of the late hour, and be too far away from home to pick up the *kinner* at a reasonable time, and he knew his horse could probably use a break.

"You weren't married to him?"

He wasn't trying to embarrass her, but he could tell by the look on her face that he'd done just that. He immediately regretted the question.

"No. I was out with him the last night I saw him, and he said he needed to stop at a friend's house before we went to dinner. We never made it to the restaurant. He and his friends offered me a glass of water, and I took it never dreaming they would put drugs in it, but they did. The last thing I remembered was Eddie taking me home and putting me in my bed because I was too dizzy to walk. When I woke up the next morning, I was naked and all alone."

Tears welled up in her eyes, and Jacob pulled her into his arms, kissing the top of her hair. "I'm so sorry he violated you in that way."

She'd made her peace with what had happened, including her decision to keep Abby in spite of how she was conceived. But that didn't mean she would ever forget the fear and hurt she felt—not to mention the shame.

Jacob lifted her chin and looked into her moist eyes as if he'd read her thoughts. "It's *his* shame, *not* yours."

She cleared her throat. "I know that now, but after what happened, I didn't think I could ever come home. When I learned I was pregnant, I moved to another town and changed my name legally. That's why my last name is Barlow. I didn't want to bring shame on my family. I led people to believe my *husband* was deceased, and I became *Englisch* to the world around me. After a few years, it came naturally."

"That doesn't explain why you named me as her *vadder.*"

Lizzie sniffed back the tears that threatened to spill, her heart racing at the confession she was about to make.

"I was still very much in love with you. I hadn't gotten over you, and since I couldn't make up a name or put Eddie's name as her father, I named you. I know I acted like a silly, immature girl by doing such a thing, but I just wasn't thinking straight at the time."

Jacob's mind was reeling, and his heart was beating so hard, he worried it would shoot out of his chest.

"If it's confessing we're doing, I have one of my own."

"What could a *gut* man like you have to confess?"

He hesitated for a moment, as if to gather his thoughts. "When you left the community, I was so devastated I tried to drown my sorrow by courting Nellie Fisher. I knew it was wrong to lead her on when I didn't feel the same, but I thought I could force myself to have a life with her—that I would learn to love her in time. She was a good woman and she deserved better than the small part of my heart, but I never got over you either. You were my first love—the only one I could ever give my heart to."

She looked up at him, disbelief in her eyes.

He ignored the shock on her face and continued before he lost his nerve. "When she died giving birth to Caleb, I was riddled with such guilt that I could barely function. My own *mamm* had to come in and help me care for him because I was no *gut* to him in the state I was in. My *familye* assumed I was grieving, but I couldn't tell them the truth. I only just told the Bishop before we were married. It was a burden that had plagued me until just a week ago before you came back to the community when I decided to shave and force myself to let go of the past. Telling the Bishop was the final step in putting my shame behind me and allowing *Gott* to forgive me."

Lizzie couldn't believe her ears. After all this time, he'd been hurting just as much as she had. "Thank you for being so honest with me, Jacob."

He picked up the reins. "We should probably head back to pick up the *kinner*. Your *aenti* is probably getting worried, and tomorrow is a long work day."

Lizzie thought about the wash she'd have to do at the B&B after doing her own family's wash, and realized it was best they go home even though she wasn't ready.

Jacob steered the buggy back toward home. "How did you manage on your own among the *Englisch* for so long?"

"I went to a trade-school after passing the GED test and became a pharmacy technician. It was good work until Eddie caught up to me. There was no denying she was his child—they look too much alike. He threatened to tell her, and take her from me if I didn't give him money for drugs. His friends even threatened to kill me if I didn't help him. But he died in a car crash a few weeks ago, and I'm sure his friends have forgotten all about me by now."

Jacob pulled her close with one arm, afraid if he let go of her, something would happen to her. He hoped she was right about the men giving up their quest for money for a dead man's debt, but he would willingly pay any amount to keep his *fraa* and *dochder* safe. It didn't matter that Abby was not his flesh and blood, and he would not shame Lizzie further by denying what the community believed about his part in conceiving her. As far as he was concerned, Abby was his *dochder* in every way that counted. He was proud of his decision to claim her as his *dochder,* for he already loved her as if she were.

CHAPTER 24

Lizzie woke up, surprised that Jacob was still cuddling her close to him. She nudged him slightly since she could see just enough in the dimly lit room to know the sun would be fully up soon. He groaned slightly, pulling her closer still. She didn't want to leave his arms, but they both had a lot of work to do without many hours of daylight to complete since the days had grown shorter.

"Stay with me just a few minutes longer." He whispered in her ear sending shivers of desire through her.

If she had her way, they wouldn't get up at all, but she was having a tough time grasping his sudden urge to lounge. Every day since they'd been married, he'd been up hours before her, yet today, he was willing to linger. Was he overtired and worn out from his added responsibility, or did he simply want to cuddle her? Either way, she wouldn't argue for long, even though she knew the delay would prolong her workday. She snuggled him, knowing the time spent with him would be worth every agonizing minute her day would extend by for staying with him.

Jacob was very aware of the desire he was invoking in her. He couldn't help feeling it himself. But he knew there was no time for the kind of closeness he desired with her, and he wasn't sure if she was ready for that yet. Not wanting to push her too far, he didn't dare kiss her, despite the magnetic pull he felt from her to do so. He wasn't sure he would be able to stop at kissing if they started anything, and there was no time for that now, no matter how much he desired to become one with her. They had a full day of work ahead of them, but that didn't stop him from wanting to hold her just a little longer.

Lizzie had to be strong for both of them. "If I stay too long, I'll want to stay longer and longer still. If we don't get up now I'm afraid we'll stay here all day."

His eyes opened slightly and he smiled at her.

"Would that be such a bad thing?"

At first thought, it wouldn't but... "We have obligations, Jacob. Not just to each other, but to the *kinner* and the community. I'm expected to help my *aenti* with Monday wash, and I believe you and Caleb are expected at the Belier's to finish the inside of the barn."

He leaned up and kissed her forehead. "You're right. I don't want you thinking I'm not a responsible man."

She tousled his curly brown hair. "I have the utmost admiration for you. After what you did for me and Abby, I could never see you as irresponsible."

He smiled at her, feeling his heart tug away with her as she lifted herself from the bed.

He was falling in love with her all over again.

ജാഗ

Lizzie couldn't keep her mind on task. Her arms went through the motions, hanging the linens on the clothesline at the B&B, but a soft blush covered her cheeks from thinking of Jacob and his desire for her. It was the same desire she felt for him, but was afraid to admit even to herself. Happiness had been a long time in coming to her, and she still feared it would leave her if she blinked too long. Abby's presence was the only thing that kept her grounded.

"Will we get home in time for *daed* to show me how to harness Snowball?"

Lizzie looked at the sun that rested high above their heads. "We have two more loads of linens to finish, and then we can go home. If we hurry and clean the last room we should be home with enough time for you to spend about thirty minutes before dinner."

"I don't have to help you cook?"

Lizzie smiled. "I think I can do without your help just this once."

Abby rushed at Lizzie with a hearty hug, and then went back to work hanging towels on the clothesline.

છા૭ક

Lizzie pulled the last piece of fried chicken from the iron skillet and placed it on the linen-clad platter. She covered it to keep it warm while she checked on her biscuits. Seeing they still had a couple of minutes, she set the table and went out to ring the bell to alert Jacob the meal was ready.

Jacob, Caleb and Abby came rushing in the door, laughing at something. It startled Lizzie, causing her to knock her hand against the hot stove when she took the biscuits out of the oven. "Oh, not again!"

Before she realized, Jacob was at her side, pulling her hand under the cold-running water in the sink. He put his arm around her and kissed her lightly on the cheek.

"I'm sorry for startling you again."

"It isn't your fault. I knew you were coming in, I just had my mind on other things."

Jacob looked her in the eye and smiled. "I've had a tough time keeping my mind on my work too."

She smiled back, losing herself in his dimples.

"I'd like it if we could take another buggy ride tomorrow night. Do you think you could arrange with Aunt Bess to stay with the *kinner?*"

"I'll ask her in the morning when I go over to clean the B&B. It'll be a short day tomorrow since she only has two guests."

Jacob's face lit up. "*Gut.* I was hoping to have some time to help Abby with Snowball. Caleb and I don't have anywhere to be tomorrow, so we will be here when you return. I'd like it if I could spend the afternoon working with her and the horse. The sooner we break him, the sooner she'll be able to ride him."

Lizzie turned off the water, satisfied she'd left her hand under the cool tap long enough. "That would make her happy. All she talks about all day is how much she wants to ride that horse. I think she'd sleep in the barn with him if we let her."

Jacob beamed at his *dochder,* and Lizzie loved him all the more for it.

CHAPTER 25

Lizzie was excited to hear that her *aenti* would watch the *kinner* so she and Jacob could take a buggy ride after the evening meal. She hoped tonight would be the night he would kiss her. As much as she tried to keep her mind on her work, she couldn't help but let her mind slip back to thoughts of Jacob. But she had work to do or she would never get home to him.

Watching Abby dust the furniture and fluff the pillows, she admired how much she fit into the Amish lifestyle so quickly, right down to the purple dress with the black apron she now wore. Since they'd gotten Snowball, she hadn't mentioned cell phones, computers or TV even once, and Lizzie wondered if her adaptation to her surroundings would stay with her.

"Are you happy now that you have a father?"

Abby looked up from her work, surprised at the question. "I thought I would miss my cell phone and TV, but I'm having a lot more fun here. And I have to admit that having a dad—*daed*—is really nice. You were right. I do love it here because everyone is nice. And I even have a few friends—Annie and Rebecca."

"Do you want to know the nice thing about your friend Annie? She's also your new cousin."

"It is nice to have a big family now. I was always lonely when it was just you and me for a family, but now I have a *daed,* and a *bruder, onkels,* and even a *grossdaddi*."

Lizzie's eyes misted over, knowing she'd made the right decision for her *dochder.*

℘℧℘℘℘℘

Lizzie watched from the fence post as Abby took her first ride on Snowball. He'd been gentle enough that Jacob felt he was ready for a rider—especially since the auctioneer claimed he'd been saddled before. Jacob was grateful that the previous owner of the seven-year-old gelding had broken him in and appeared to have treated him well, creating a gentle animal fit for his *dochder.*

Abby felt very comfortable on Snowball, as though she was meant for horseback riding. She felt like the luckiest girl in the world to have such a nice new *daed* to get her a horse of her own. She knew her friend, Rachel, would be envious of such a gift, and she intended to write to her—snail-mail, of course, just as soon she got the chance. Her *mamm* had tried to explain to her how much more satisfying getting a real letter in the mail can be, but she was still a little unsure of it. The important thing, though, was that she would help her to keep in contact with her best friend.

Jacob continued to walk beside Snowball, ensuring Abby's safety since the horse was new to her. "You're doing a *gut* job of learning. Snowball seems to have been made just for you."

Abby leaned in and stroked Snowball's silky neck.

"Can I braid his mane with red ribbons and put jingle bells around his neck for Christmas?"

Jacob laughed heartily. "That sounds like a *gut* idea. If we get him trained in time, we can have him pull the sleigh."

Abby's eyes grew wide. "You have a sleigh?"

Jacob smiled at her excitement. "*Jah*. We take the sleigh to visit neighbors at Christmas. It goes easier in the snow than the buggy."

Abby giggled, delighting Jacob.

"I can't wait for it to snow!"

Jacob could see that raising a *dochder* was going to be a lot different than raising Caleb—especially since she'd been raised as an *Englischer*. He might have missed her first steps, and other firsts in her young life, but he knew there were plenty of "firsts" ahead of them to look forward to as a *familye*—including her first sleigh ride.

And he could hardly wait.

CHAPTER 26

Jacob was eager to get his *fraa* home after their buggy ride—especially since Aunt Bess offered to keep the *kinner* overnight. He had to admit that he was nervous to be alone with Lizzie, even though they'd slept in the same bed together since their marriage. But this was different. They would have no responsibilities except to each other for the entire night. But first, he would enjoy the remainder of their buggy ride together by the light of the harvest moon.

Lizzie reached for Jacob's hand and leaned into his shoulder. She didn't mind the chill in the air; her thoughts of Jacob were keeping her cheeks pretty heated. The quilt that spread across their laps was the very quilt her *mamm* had made for her. She wanted to use it once before giving it to Abby for her bed. It was made for her at Abby's same age, and Lizzie felt it important that she have something from the *grossmammi* she would never get to meet.

Jacob clenched her cold fingers in his. "Are you warm enough?"

"I'm a little cold, but I'd like to stop for a minute alongside the road to gaze at the stars if that's alright with you."

"*Jah.*" Jacob pulled the buggy to the side of the dirt road and gazed upward. "The sky is full of stars tonight."

Lizzie nuzzled in a little closer, and Jacob put his arm around her.

"I really missed the stars living in the city. The view out here is so bright, whereas the stars are hard to see against the city lights."

Lizzie tilted her head up. "There must be a billion of them out tonight."

Jacob watched her as she smiled at the stars. She was so beautiful against the moonlight, he wondered if it was too soon to kiss her. He loved her more than he ever thought he could, and didn't think he could stand to wait even another moment for her full lips to touch his.

She turned to him then. "Are you still angry with me?"

Jacob's heart caught in throat. He wasn't expecting such a question. "Why would I be angry with you?"

"Because you were forced to marry me!"

Jacob pulled both of her hands in his and turned to face her. "No one forced me. I did it willingly. At first I thought it was to keep from being excommunicated. But when I saw how much you and Abby needed me I realized that maybe Caleb and I needed you too."

Lizzie swallowed the lump that tried to invade her throat. "How do we make this work when it really seems like we used each other to stay in the community?"

Jacob pulled her close enough to smell the flowery fragrance of her hair. "Because I never stopped loving you! And it took being forced into a marriage to make me realize it."

Lizzie giggled. "So you admit to being forced to marrying me?"

"Yes! But that doesn't mean I'm not *froh.*"

Lizzie looked him in the eye, noticing for the first time just how handsome he really was. She'd not been able to really look at him since they'd been married, and she realized she was happy too.

Jacob cupped her cold cheeks in his warm hands and pulled her close, placing his lips on hers. Leaning into his advances, she tasted his sweet kisses, feeling like they were drips of honey on her tongue.

ꙮ

Lizzie slipped under the quilt and waited for Jacob to finish taking care of the horse and buggy. She put her fingers to her lips, remembering the way Jacob's lips felt when they'd touched hers. They'd shared one kiss when they were younger, but it was nothing like the passionate kiss they'd just shared only a few minutes ago.

Jacob entered the bedroom, causing Lizzie's pulse to race. It made her so nervous she jumped from the bed and stood in front of the window. Jacob stood behind her, folding his arms around her.

"Is something wrong?"

Everything is right for the first time in a very long time. So why am I so afraid?

She turned around swiftly and looked him in the eye, her mouth slightly agape as though she wanted to say something and forgot midsentence. He dragged his fingers through her long, brown hair and lowered his mouth to hers. Love surged through him as he drew her so close he could barely breathe, but he feared he would lose his breath altogether if he let her slip from his grasp. She welcomed the kiss as his mouth swept over hers with sweet desperation. She knew that desperation well; it had been building in her soul for the past ten years, and escalated during the week while she waited for him to claim her as his. She stumbled backward, pulling him toward the bed where she could give herself to him with reckless abandon. Jacob was her one true love, and she would have him forever this time around.

CHAPTER 27

One year later...

"I can't do this anymore, Jacob. You're going to have to ask someone else!"

Jacob smoothed Lizzie's damp hair from her face, and watched the midwife's face for the signal.

"One more push, Lizzie. Just one more, I promise."

Exhausted, Lizzie pushed once more, feeling the pressure of her *boppli's* head emerging. She hadn't struggled this much giving birth to Abby. Was something wrong?

"Stop pushing for a minute and let me ease out the shoulders. This one looks like he's built like his *daed.*"

Jacob squeezed Lizzie's hand and whispered in her ear to distract her from pushing for a minute.

"I've never been more in *lieb* with you than right now, Lizzie."

Lizzie giggled, tears streaming down her cheeks when her *boppli* emerged. He was beautiful, with a full head of curly brown hair like Jacob's. The midwife wiped his face and handed him to Lizzie for examination.

He was perfect in every way.

Suddenly, another contraction assailed Lizzie, causing her to let out a scream. Jacob lifted the *boppli* from her arms and stood up, fear directed at the midwife.

"I think we have another *boppli* trying to make its way into your *familye.*"

Lizzie pushed herself up on her elbows. "What do you mean another one? You only heard one heartbeat!"

"Sometimes these things get missed. Get ready to push so we can deliver this little one."

Lizzie laid back, a thousand thoughts whirling in her head, but all she had time to concentrate on were the contractions causing her to push another *boppli* from her. One good push and the next one was born, screaming loudly.

Lizzie held her arms out for her new *dochder.*

The midwife listened to Lizzie's abdomen through the stethoscope. "That was the last one, I promise!"

Lizzie smiled at Jacob, who held his son, while she held his *dochder*—his real *dochder*. Lizzie had to admit she'd been a little afraid this day would come.

She'd been hoping for a boy her entire pregnancy, concerned that Abby would no longer feel like Jacob's *dochder* if he had one of his own. But here she was, faced with reality, and wondered how her husband was feeling.

When the midwife finished with Lizzie, she took newborn Samuel from Jacob's arms and went across the room to clean him up while Lizzie and Jacob picked out a name for their *dochder*.

"What do you think of the name Rachel? That was my *mamm's* name."

Jacob kissed Lizzie gently. "I think it's a perfect name."

Lifting her chin gently, he kissed her again. "Is something troubling you?"

Lizzie chose her words carefully. "I wonder what you're thinking now that I've truly given you a *dochder.*"

Jacob smoothed back Lizzie's hair and kissed her on the forehead. "I'll always cherish Abby, and I couldn't love her any more if she was my own flesh and blood. I'm sure you feel the same for Caleb."

Lizzie frowned. "You're right. I do. But Abby isn't your real *dochder*, and this *boppli* is your flesh and blood."

Jacob smiled. "You gave me a *dochder* when I married you, and I gave you a son. Now we've been blessed with another one of each, and for that, I will always love you."

"I love you too, Jacob."

Lizzie and Jacob couldn't stop smiling. They each now held a newborn—their *bopplin*—made from their love.

**PLEASE CONTINUE READING...
SNEAK PEEK OF
BOOK TWO in this series...
Amish Winter Wonderland
Two full chapters on the next page...

AMISH WINTER WONDERLAND

CHAPTER 1

"Do you even *like* boys?"

Lillian Stoltzfus didn't like the tone her younger sister, Hannah, was using—or her implications.

"That isn't funny. Of course I like boys! They just don't like me!"

Hannah held up her hand apologetically. "I didn't mean that the way it sounded. But you have to admit that it appears you *want* to be a spinster."

"That's a mean thing to say, Hannah"

"Maybe you need to make yourself a little more available to the *menner* when we have working bees. You have a lot to offer a husband since you have your own bakery that *daed* built for you. It's on your own land and everything. What man wouldn't want you for his *fraa*?"

Lillian sighed. "You know he only built the bakery on the land adjoining our farm so he could keep an eye on me—that, and the fact he only had *dochdern*. We both know if he'd had the son he wanted, I probably wouldn't have any of it. He's saving that land to sell to a potential suitor for me! But that's exactly the problem, I'm afraid. The *menner* in this community don't seem to want a strong, independent woman for a *fraa.*"

Hannah pinched her brow against the hazy October sun as they hung the last of the wash on the clothes line. Being the last day in October, it was already nearly too chilly to hang wash on the line, but the two of them made the decision, despite the fact their fingers were so cold, they could barely grasp the wet clothes.

Hannah winked at her. "Don't get discouraged. You aren't going to end up becoming a spinster if I can help it."

Lillian picked up the wicker hamper and walked toward the house. "Of course I will—especially since I'm about to turn twenty-five. But at least with my baking business, I won't be a burden to *mamm* and *daed.*"

"You're forgetting one thing. There *is* one man in the community still unmarried who's about your age."

Lillian stopped in her tracks. "If you're going to try to sell me on Seth Miller again, it won't work! He's five years older than me. It's obvious he doesn't want a *fraa,* or he'd already have one. Besides, he's way too quiet. He never talks to me when he comes into the bakery—ever. I take that as a sign he just isn't interested in me."

If the truth be told, Lillian had been interested in him for the past year, ever since he started coming into the bakery on a regular basis. But though he would sometimes linger, he never said very much, especially nothing that would give her the impression he liked her. She was hopelessly infatuated with him, and it frustrated her that she was alone in her feelings. She couldn't even be sure she could consider Seth a friend because friends usually talked more than the two of them did.

Hannah pushed out her lower lip. "Or he's just shy. Lillian, you're much prettier than I am. How could he *not* want you for his *fraa?* A man would have to be blind not to see how perfect you are. *"

Lillian turned her back on her *schweschder.* "Don't insult me, Hannah. We both know you inherited *mamm's* beauty. And no man is that shy. I think he has too much responsibility to his *daed*. Maybe that's why his *schweschder* ran away all those years ago—because of Hiram Miller's strict parenting."

Hannah stayed on her heels. "I'm not going to criticize the man's parenting, but I'll agree he does seem to work poor Seth to the bone. His loyalty to his *daed* is honorable—that's a *gut* quality in a man. As far as you not being pretty, maybe if Seth saw you in something other than work dresses, he might take notice. Every time he comes into the bakery, your hair is always messy, and you're wearing flour-covered work dresses, and your underarms are sweaty. You might as well wear *Daed's* trousers and suspenders for all the feminine quality you display."

Lillian turned sharply to confront her younger sibling. "That's because I'm always working! Maybe if you worked as hard as I do you'd understand that. Seth has seen me at the church services in my Sunday dress, and he doesn't take notice. What have you to say about that?"

"I'd say I'm going to make you a new dress! You haven't made a new dress in at least two years, and you wear the same dull, worn out brown dress every service. You would look nice in a blue. Maybe that would attract his attention. And the blue would go nicely with your eyes."

Lillian pursed her lips. "Such talk of vanity. You better not let *daed* hear you talking like that or he will make you have a meeting with Bishop Troyer."

Hannah waved a careless hand at her. "I'll begin your dress today after I go into town with *daed*. I will get the most beautiful blue material for a dress, and you can wear it to the singing on Saturday."

Lillian continued on her path to the kitchen door. "I have never attended a singing, and I have no intention of attending one now. I'm too old."

"You are not too old. I want you to come to the singing with me and Jonathon Graber. I'll have him bring his cousin, Henry, and we'll make Seth jealous."

"First of all, Seth will likely not attend the singing because he's older than I am—he's thirty! Second, Henry is barely twenty, so I'm way too old for him. And third—when did you start dating Jonathon?"

Hannah smiled. "We've been sneaking around for months, and you would know that if you didn't work all the time."

Lillian narrowed her eyes. "You think I want to work so much? I didn't ask for that bakery—let's not forget that."

"You don't have to take it out on me. But promise you won't tell *daed* about Jonathon; I don't want him interfering."

"So my little *boppli schweschder* is to be married before me. I'm going to be the last one to be married in the community—if I'm lucky enough to marry at all!"

ℯ⌘ℬ

Seth entered the small baking house nestled on the main road at the far edge of the Stoltzfus farm, and spotted Lillian immediately. His heart thumped in his chest, and heat crawled up his neck when her blue eyes pierced his. She was waiting on an *Englisch* woman, but she paused to look at him at the sound of the bells on the door that jingled his presence. He hated those bells that caught him unaware every time he entered the small bakery, forgetting to avert his eyes in time to avoid eye-contact with Lillian. It caught him off guard every time, but yet for some reason, he couldn't pull his eyes away from her.

He tried not to stare as she pushed stray, dark blonde tendrils behind her ear with the back of her flour-covered hand. A light dusting of sheen illuminated her cheeks, indicating she'd been hard at work preparing his special order—the same order he picked up every Monday and every Thursday for the past year. He'd come in every week, and still he found it difficult to converse with Lillian, though he'd been hopelessly infatuated with her for some time. If not for all the work he did around the farm, his waistline would be a tell-tale sign of his feelings for Lillian.

At twenty-nine, he'd missed his chance to court in his teenage years and his twenties due to extra responsibilities on his *daed's* farm. And now, he felt socially awkward from lack of experience at a time when he'd felt more confident, but his youthful bravery had faltered with time. He had no hope for a suitable mate, feeling he'd become set in his ways and wouldn't know how to act even if the situation presented itself. Working long hours on the farm, sometimes alone, had rendered him speechless in Lillian's presence, lest he open his mouth and make a fool of himself by tripping over his words.

No, it was best to keep as quiet as possible around her, and not risk gazing upon her beautiful face too long. Though he knew it was pointless to hope for a life with her, it didn't stop him from wanting to take her for a buggy ride.

❧❦

Lillian tried not to let her voice falter as Seth stepped forward to pick up his order. She'd added a couple of pumpkin muffins to his regular order, and now she wished she hadn't done it. It was a bold move on her part, but she had to do something to get his attention once for all. Though she now second-guessed her assertiveness, it was too late to remove them from the closed box. He'd think it un-Christian of her if she removed items from his box after he'd already paid. She'd put them in as a gift, and there was no taking them back. Thankfully, he wouldn't discover them until he reached home.

It was all Hannah's fault for planting ideas in her head about Seth, and making her think she had a chance with him. And now she was trying to win his attention with baked goods? Heat crept up her cheeks as she felt like a fool for thinking Seth would show an interest in her over a couple of pumpkin muffins. He'd been ordering from her bakery since she opened it last year, and he'd never offered her any indication he was interested in anything beyond the pies and pastries she baked for him and his *daed* every week. But it was Seth's loyalty to his *daed* that kept him from having a life of his own, and that didn't give Lillian confidence that she could ever win his heart— not that she was sure if she even wanted to. To open herself up to him could mean heartache, and she wasn't sure she could risk it.

What she still couldn't figure out was why Seth's silence irritated her so much today. Perhaps the surprise in his box of baked goods would spark a conversation from his all-business tone when he came back in on Thursday.

She could only hope…

CHAPTER 2

Hiram Miller sat down with his cup of *kaffi* and a pumpkin muffin from the bakery. He wondered why Seth had gotten the extra goody, but as he bit into the moist treat, he had no complaints.

Seth came in from the morning milking and stared at the confection in his *daed's* hand. "Where did that come from?"

Hiram held up the muffin for inspection. "It was in the box you got from the bakery. Didn't you check the order yesterday when you got it?"

Seth went to the box that rested on the counter, and saw the other muffin and reached inside to retrieve it. "I didn't think to check it. Miss Stoltzfus has never gotten our order wrong. Maybe she was having a sale, or they're day-old and she was giving them away. But in case it was a mistake, I'll make up the difference when I go back on Thursday."

Hiram chuckled. "I'm sure she'll appreciate that. In the meantime, I'm going to enjoy this muffin. No sense in letting it go to waste."

Seth poured himself a cup of *kaffi* and joined his *daed* at the table and decided he would do the same. One bite of the delicious muffin sent his senses straight to Heaven. Not only was Lillian beautiful, she could bake like an angel. He looked across the table at his *daed,* who sat silent, and wondered what it would be like to have Lillian sitting across the table from him chattering in her pleasant, joyful tone with him. He was lonely, and he had been for a long time. Was it too late to hope he could ever win her heart? One thing he was sure of; it would never happen if he couldn't get up enough courage to talk to her.

ഇൻൽ

"Hold still or I'm going to stick you with a pin."

Lillian fidgeted on purpose. She didn't want to be on display in front of her *mamm* and *daed* while

Hannah measured the bottom of her new dress for the hem.

"I'm being as still as I can, but you've had me standing on this chair so long I'm getting dizzy."

Hannah looked up at her and scoffed. "That's a fib, Lillian, and you know it. Confess right now!"

Lillian narrowed her eyes, and crossed her arms. "I will do no such thing. You're making me feel uncomfortable with all this attention. I don't need a new dress."

Beth Stoltzfus looked up from her mending and admired the blue dress on her *dochder*. "Yes you do. And that color is perfect for you. I get tired of seeing you in the same dull brown and gray dresses all the time. The brighter color will do you some *gut*."

Lillian's cheeks heated. "But *mamm,* this is the color for marrying. And it's November now. I don't want to wear this color during wedding season. The entire community will believe I am fishing for a husband!"

Thankfully, her *daed* hadn't looked up from his reading with her comment.

Her *mamm* tipped her head. "I could see them thinking that. But since when do you let gossip control what you do? It makes me *froh* to know that I have a *dochder* who is strong enough to withstand the pressures of the rest of the youth."

Lillian conceded. There was nothing to gain from openly disagreeing with her *mamm,* and Hannah was determined to make her social life her personal responsibility until her match-making efforts were successful. Perhaps when she failed and Seth failed to show interest in her, Hannah would eventually give up. If not, she was in for a long winter.

ॐ

Lillian looked at the time, noting that Seth was later than usual in picking up his order—not that she was keeping track of him or anything. But he was a creature of habit, and he was never this late, and there was no sign of him. She stared out the bakery window, wondering what could be keeping him, as she dialed the phone to her *daed's* barn.

He picked up on the fourth ring. "Efram Stoltzfus here."

Lillian cleared her throat. "*Daed,* would you mind hitching the small buggy for me so I can make a delivery?"

"If it's far I can drive you. It will be dark soon."

Lillian could feel the blush creeping up her cheeks. She didn't want her *daed* tagging along, and having Seth think she was a *boppli.*

"No. it's just down the road to the Miller's. They never picked up their order and I don't want it to turn stale."

"I should have it ready by the time you walk down to the barn." He hung up without another word.

୬୦୯ଓ

Lillian felt her nerves jangle as she drove the small buggy down the lane toward Seth's farm. She wasn't sure if she hoped he was there or not, but she had to admit she was a little concerned about why he hadn't shown up for his order. As she pulled into the yard, she spotted Hiram Miller mending a section of fence near the barn.

He tipped his hat when she exited the buggy, the box of baked goods in her hands. "Evening, Miss Stoltzfus."

"*Gut* evening, Mr. Miller. When I closed the bakery, I realized Seth had not yet picked up your order. I hope you don't mind I brought it over, but I didn't want it to get stale, and I figured you would want the pie for your evening meal."

He took the box from her. "*Denki.* Seth had to go over and help his *schweschder,* Lizzie and her husband. I expect him back any time if you'd like to wait for him."

Hiram smiled knowingly, making Lillian worry that he could read her anxiousness in knowing Seth's whereabouts.

She shrugged. "I don't need to see him for anything. He can settle his bill when I see him on Tuesday. Have a *gut* night, Mr. Miller."

He tipped his hat again, the corners of his mouth forming a smile. Lillian could feel the heat reaching her cheeks, and she bolted away without another word. Did he know how she felt about his son? She prayed Seth wouldn't think she was being too forward by bringing his order to his *haus*.

You can purchase a copy of Amish Winter Wonderland from the same online store you purchased this book.

Thanks for reading.

http://livingstonhallpublishers.blogspot.com/

Under the Mulberry Tree: Book Three

Jacob's Daughter series

An Amish Christmas

Coming November, 2012

Amish Winter Wonderland: Book Two

Next in the Jacob's Daughter series

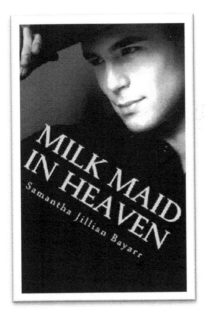

Christian Romance

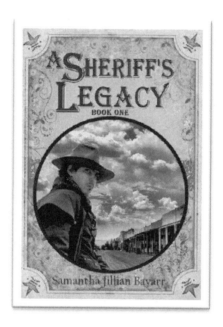

Book One

Christian/Historical Romance

Made in the USA
Charleston, SC
31 August 2012